Wealth Starts Here

Gregory A. Thomas

Published by Gregory A. Thomas Enterprises, 2025.

WEALTH STARTS HERE

First edition. July 18, 2025.

ISBN: 979-8231486533

Written by Gregory A. Thomas.

Dedication

To my Financial Wellness students—

You are the reason I wrote this book. Your hunger for knowledge, your discipline to show up, and your courage to break generational cycles are the truest form of wealth I've ever witnessed. I watched you turn concrete walls into classrooms and scarcity into strategy. You reminded me that power begins the moment we decide to learn.

To Major Alexis Stewart, Captain Michael Sherwood, Teacher Daniel Garcia, Warden Shane Stucker, and Associate Warden Jennifer Malebranche—

Thank you for believing in rehabilitation over routine. For creating space where others might've seen obstacles. For trusting me with the sacred task of teaching behind the wire. Your leadership didn't just allow me to continue my purpose—it multiplied it.

Because of all of you, this book exists.

And because of this book, others will rise.

With honor,

Dr. Gregory A. Thomas

Big Tex

Foreword

By Governor Rick Perry

Former Governor of Texas | United States Secretary of Energy (Ret.)

I've had the honor of knowing a great many men in my life—soldiers, governors, business leaders, pastors, and policymakers. But few have earned my admiration quite like Dr. Gregory A. Thomas. His life, his journey, and his impact stand as a living testimony to the idea that greatness isn't given—it's built.

Wealth Starts Here isn't just a book about money. It's a blueprint for discipline, legacy, and financial clarity in a world that too often leaves people guessing. Dr. Thomas strips away the fluff and hands the reader something rare: truth backed by lived wisdom.

What sets Gregory apart isn't just his knowledge of economics or markets. It's his unwavering commitment to making sure that those who've been counted out know how to count themselves back in. Whether you're starting with nothing, starting over, or simply starting late, this book shows you how to win—and win with integrity.

I've watched this man pour into young people, formerly incarcerated men, first-time entrepreneurs, and everyday working Americans. He doesn't just talk about wealth. He teaches how to build it from the ground up—starting with mindset, strategy, and heart.

This book isn't theory. It's road-tested. And it's needed now more than ever.

Gregory, I'm proud to call you my friend. I'm even prouder to witness how your life continues to prove that faith, grit, and financial literacy are a combination that can change families—and reshape futures.

To every reader holding this book in your hands: you're holding a set of keys. What you unlock is up to you.

Rick Perry,
Former Governor of Texas
Personal Friend and Proud Supporter

Foreword 2

By William "Bill" Sonju

It's been said that wealth is more than money—it's a mindset, a set of principles, and most importantly, a legacy. Over the past decade, I've had the distinct honor of walking alongside Dr. Gregory A. Thomas as we've taught those principles behind prison walls. Together, we've seen firsthand the hunger for knowledge, the spark of transformation, and the undeniable truth that freedom begins in the mind long before it's experienced in the world.

Gregory and I met over ten years ago, united by a shared mission: to bring financial literacy to some of the most overlooked and underestimated individuals in our society. From classrooms deep inside Colorado's correctional facilities to late-night lesson planning sessions, our friendship has been forged in the trenches of real change. And let me tell you—Gregory is the real deal. He doesn't just teach wealth—he embodies it. Not the flashy kind you see on social media, but the durable, time-tested kind built on faith, discipline, service, and vision.

Wealth Starts Here isn't just a title—it's a declaration. It's a rallying cry for first-timers, dreamers, and the determined. It's a resource for the incarcerated man planning for reentry, the single mother working two jobs, the young graduate with student debt and ambition, and the lifelong hustler ready to flip the script.

What makes this book different is its heart. Gregory doesn't just hand you financial formulas—he walks you through mindset shifts, foundational truths, and real-life application with clarity, compassion, and conviction. Every chapter echoes the same empowering message we've preached behind those barbed-wire fences: you are not your past; you are your potential—and your financial future is yours to claim.

As someone who has spent years alongside Gregory in this fight for financial education and human dignity, I can tell you—this book will change lives. Not because it's filled with hype or promises, but because it's grounded in truth, written from lived experience, and delivered with the fierce love of a man who knows what it means to rise on purpose.

— **William "Bill" Sonju**

Financial Literacy Advocate, Colorado Prison Program Educator, Friend and Brother-in-the-Fight

Advance Praise for Wealth Starts Here: Investing for First-Timers, Dreamers, and the Determined

"This book is a wake-up call for anyone who's ever said, 'I'll figure money out later.' Dr. Thomas breaks it down with clarity, conviction, and cultural intelligence. Wealth Starts Here belongs on every young investor's shelf."

— Vanessa Liu, CFA, Founder of NextGen Capital Partners

"In a world full of financial gimmicks and get-rich-quick noise, Gregory Thomas delivers wisdom that's grounded, tested, and powerful. This book is a blueprint for building lasting wealth—especially for those starting with more grit than capital."

— Eric D. Hamilton, Managing Director, Harvest View Wealth Advisors

"This is more than a book—it's a financial revival. Gregory Thomas has given the streets, the prisons, and the boardrooms something they've all been waiting for: a guide that speaks truth with strategy. Wealth Starts Here is a movement."

— Tasha Green, Financial Educator & Host of "Money Mindset Mondays"

"Dr. Thomas has written a financial classic that speaks the language of the underserved while delivering the principles of the elite. Wealth Starts Here isn't just smart—it's revolutionary."

— Kevin Marks, Former Goldman Sachs VP and Founder of Reclaim Wealth Institute

"From trust fund wisdom to street-smart strategy, this book bridges worlds. It's rare to find a guide that empowers the incarcerated, the entrepreneur, and the everyday American all at once. But this one does—and it does it flawlessly."

— Darryl Mathis, CEO of Equity First Financial Group

CHAPTER 1: WHY I INVEST

A Letter from Gregory A. Thomas

(As originally published in Big Tex's Financial Times, June 15, 2022)

By Carla Mendoza

I. THE SANCTUARY OF STEEL

The elevator hissed open like a bullet sliding into a chamber. No fanfare, no corporate chimes—just the silent exhale of hydraulics parting steel. Carla Mendoza stepped onto the trading floor of Carbonado Capital Investments and felt the air tighten around her. Concrete floors, exposed ductwork, the scent of leather and espresso hanging thick as Gulf Coast humidity. Light fell in slants through floor-to-ceiling windows, cutting across Bloomberg terminals where young men and women moved in the reverent silence of a cathedral.

At the center of it all stood Dr. Gregory A. Thomas.

He faced a triptych of glowing screens, the cobalt wash of bond yields painting his profile in cold light. His trademark obsidian cowboy hat cast a shadow that sharpened the angles of his face—a face that gave nothing away. Not tension, not triumph. Only the absolute stillness of a predator poised between breaths. An analyst in a faded band t-shirt approached, murmuring numbers. Thomas didn't turn.

"Sell December wheat. 500 contracts. Scale in at $842.50 resistance."

His voice was gravel-road rough, the command leaving no room for hesitation. The analyst vanished. Only then did Thomas pivot. Python-skin boots struck concrete like hammer falls as he closed the distance between them. No suit jacket softened his frame—just charcoal denim and a black blazer cut with military precision. When his hand closed around Carla's, the pressure was deliberate, testing.

"Carla Mendoza." He released her hand. "Big Tex reads your column. You don't flinch."

"And you don't smile," she countered, flipping open her notebook.

A ghost of something—not amusement, not quite—flickered in his eyes. "Smiles cost time. Time costs alpha." He swept his Stetson off and placed it crown-down on a steel table. The gesture felt like uncasing a weapon. "Ask your questions. But know this: I don't do inspiration. I do infrastructure."

◈ Tex Talks: Welcome to the Arena

The first time you walk into a serious trading floor, it feels like church—only the deity is discipline. No one's waiting to inspire you. They're watching to see if you crack. The market doesn't need your dreams. It demands your discipline.

II. THE TRUST FUND TRAP

"They call you 'Big Tex' behind your back," Carla began. "Is it the hat? The returns? Or the fact you walked away from a fortune?"

Thomas didn't sit. He paced behind the table, a caged wolf circling territory he'd already claimed. "My grandfather died when I was twenty-one. Left me four point two million dollars. Stocks. Bonds. A chunk of a failing West Texas oil field." He paused, fingertips brushing the brim of his hat. "I wired it all back to the family trust six months later."

Carla's pen froze. "Why?"

"Because inheritance is a gilded cage," he said, the words stripped bare. "That money came with strings—board seats for cousins who couldn't balance a checkbook, investments in rigs sucking dust. It wasn't capital. It was collateral against my freedom."

He stopped pacing, locked eyes with her. "Wealth isn't a number in a ledger, Ms. Mendoza. It's sovereignty. The day I handed back that trust fund was the day I started building something that couldn't be taken away. Something that couldn't be given."

The Garage Days:

"Bought a '97 Ford F-250 for $3,200. Slept in it for six months outside the Mercantile Library," Thomas said, his voice flat. "Why? Because libraries have free Wi-Fi and SEC filings. Traded oil futures on a Thinkorswim account. Woke up at 4 AM to track Asian market opens. Showered at truck stops."

He pulled a folded paper from his blazer—a faded brokerage statement dated January 5, 2011. "Turned

$18,437 into $412,000 in fourteen months. No leverage. Just volatility and nerve."

◈ Tex Talks: Don't Confuse Rich with Free

I wasn't broke—I had millions in my name. But I was a prisoner to everyone else's version of success. True wealth isn't what you inherit. It's what you control, and what you can walk away from. Freedom costs. Pay up front.

Carbonado's Genesis:

Five years later, the firm had clawed its way into the eight-figure range. Today, it manages over $700 million in assets—not through pedigree, but precision.

His rules were etched into the culture:

1. No Ivy Leaguers. "Harvard teaches theory. The streets teach survival. I want traders who've smelled blood."
2. No real-time data until Year 3. "We used Yahoo Finance and yesterday's Barron's. Distraction is the enemy of edge."
3. Profit shares, not salaries. "No skin in the game? Get out."

He nodded toward the kid in grease-stained jeans Carla had noticed earlier. "See him? Walked in here eighteen months ago with eight hundred fourteen dollars and a chip on his shoulder. Last month he cleared two hundred seventeen thousand dollars trading soybean futures. Not because he's a genius. Because he follows the process."

III. THE 2014 MORTGAGE MASSACRE

"Process?" Carla raised an eyebrow. "Is that what you called shorting Lennar Corp into oblivion?"

For the first time, something like warmth touched Thomas's expression. "September 2014. Every hedge fund clown was chasing tech IPOs. Alibaba had just gone public. Froth was thick as East Texas mud. I smelled something else."

He leaned forward, palms flat on the steel table. "The Fed was pumping sunshine about 'housing recovery.' CNBC parroted it. But I'd pulled delinquency reports from county courthouses in Arizona, Nevada, Florida. Subprime mortgages were imploding. Twenty-two percent spike in defaults. Lennar Corp—biggest homebuilder in the Sun Belt—was sitting on a mountain of bad paper."

Carla scribbled furiously. "But their stock was climbing."

"Climbing?" Thomas's laugh was a short, sharp bark. "It was parabolic. Pure delusion. So I bought puts. Three thousand contracts. Strike price five-fifty."

"That was... what? Four hundred thousand in premium?"

"Four-twelve kay," he corrected. "Thirty-eight percent of my fund's capital. My risk manager quit. Said I'd bankrupt us."

"What did you tell him?"

Thomas's gaze didn't waver. "I told him fear is a tax on returns. Pay it or get out."

The Execution Log:

- October 23, 2014: Lennar misses Q3 earnings. EPS $0.75 vs. $0.82 expected. Stock drops 9%.
- November 5, 2014: FBI subpoenas mortgage documents. Stock drifts down 4%.
- November 7, 2014: Wall Street Journal leaks criminal probe into appraisal fraud. LEN opens down 17%.

"We exited at nine-ten per contract," Thomas said. "Two point seven-eight million profit. Six hundred seventy-five percent return."

◈ Tex Talks: Risk Isn't the Enemy

Playing it safe never made history. I risked 38% of the fund that day. Why? Because conviction isn't enough—you need execution. The data backed it, the math proved it, and the streets confirmed it. Fear costs more than failure.

IV. THE BOOTSTRAP BOOTCAMP

"Is that why you started the South Dallas initiative?" Carla asked. "To find kids who don't know how to flinch?"

Thomas's eyes hardened to glacial ice. "Talent is universal. Access isn't. I found Jamal Reynolds in a public library basement. Sixteen years old. Foster kid. He was hunched over a monitor older than he was, scrolling through Tesla's 10-K on the SEC's EDGAR database."

The Bootcamp Rules:

- 4:30 AM arrivals. "Markets open at eight. Be ready."
- SEC filings only. "Free data beats paid opinions every time."
- Minimum $5,000 positions. "No paper trading. Skin in the game or stay home."

"February. Two years ago. Jamal's reading AMD's annual. He looks up: 'Gross margin's up 3%, R&D spiked 22%. That sustainable?' I point to footnote C, cash flow. He sees it. 'Operating cash down 18%. They're bleeding.' That's when I knew—he got it."

Jamal's First Trade:

January $15 calls on AMD. $5,000 in. Sold for $74,000. Jamal started Wharton that fall. His first paper? "Footnotes & Freight Trains: How Contrarian Data Mining Uncovers Alpha."

◈ Tex Talks: You Can't Coach Hunger

You either want it or you don't. I'm not here to babysit ambition. If you're willing to dig through SEC filings when your friends are at the mall—you're ready for this game. That's where wealth starts in obsession, not convenience.

V. THE SHADOW AT THE DOOR

Carla sensed the shift before she saw it. The energy in the room tightened. Thomas's gaze flicked toward the frosted glass doors. A man in a cheap suit stood there, arms crossed. Federal marshal badge clipped to his belt.

"Dr. Thomas," Carla kept her voice level. "What's your greatest fear?"

His knuckles whitened. For a heartbeat—just one—the mask slipped. Not fear. Fury.

"Complacency," he said. "Wealth without purpose is a tomb."

He lifted the Stetson and locked it into place.

"They'll tell you money corrupts," he said. "Bullshit. Weakness corrupts. Money just amplifies who you already are."

He walked toward the marshal. The glass hissed open. Then sealed shut behind him.

VI. AUTHOR'S COMMENTARY: THE UNBREAKABLE CORE

(Present Day: Gregory A. Thomas)

Re-reading Carla Mendoza's words now—from a Colorado prison cell—I see the arrogance. Not of ego, but of certainty. I knew my system worked. I didn't know how fiercely that system would be tested.

But Carla captured the raw nerve of truth:

> Wealth isn't capital. It's captivity to nothing.

When the marshals took my blazer and handed me prison grays, they took nothing essential. I still possessed:

- The Lennar Corp Playbook (See Ch. 5: Risk & Reward)

- Jamal's EDGAR Database Drills (See Ch. 6: The Language of Ownership)
- The Soybean Trader's Discipline (See Ch. 14: Building Your Starter Portfolio)

These tools don't require a trading floor. They require only a mind forged in the fires of conviction—a mind that trades opportunity, not excuses.

The First Week Inside:

No Bloomberg. No Thinkorswim. Just a steel bunk and a dog-eared copy of Barron's from the prison library—three weeks old. I opened it to page B3. Pfizer had just raised its dividend 6%. Stock hadn't moved yet in the delayed data. I used my first 20-minute call: "Buy 1,500 PFE. Hold five years." Two years later? 34% gain + dividends. Slow motion beats no motion.

They took my freedom.

They couldn't touch my sovereignty.

◈ Tex Talks: If You've Got a Mind, You've Got a Market

They can take the screens, the suit, the freedom. But they can't take the one asset you build brick by brick—your investor's mind. You don't need a broker. You need belief, data, and execution.

This book is the blueprint for yours.

Turn the page. Let's begin.

Chapter 2: The Truth About Wealth (And Why You Were Never Taught It)

You weren't meant to be poor.

Let's just start there. Not to sound harsh, not to trigger guilt or shame — but to confront a lie that's kept far too many people stuck.

The truth is, poverty isn't always a condition — sometimes it's a strategy. A system. A profitable business model. And for generations, that model has depended on one thing: your ignorance.

That's why most people were never taught about wealth — because knowledge is expensive to those who profit from your lack of it.

The Hidden Curriculum

You went to school, right? They taught you algebra, U.S. history, maybe even the square root of 144. But did anyone teach you:

- How to invest in a mutual fund?
- What compound interest really means?
- Why the wealthy buy assets instead of collecting paychecks?

Of course not. Because the system isn't designed to produce wealth builders. It's designed to produce workers. W-2 earners. Dependents.

And here's what you need to understand:

There's a difference between education and indoctrination.

Education liberates. Indoctrination limits. And when it comes to money, most people received the latter.

They taught you how to earn money, but not how to own anything.

They taught you how to budget, but not how to build.

They taught you to spend responsibly, but not how to invest aggressively.

They kept you trained for jobs, not built for freedom.

So What Is Wealth?

Let's break this down.

Wealth is not just money. It's not your car, your paycheck, your house, or even your business income.

Wealth is measured in:

- Time – How long can you live without working?
- Ownership – What do you control that appreciates in value?
- Freedom – How much of your life is dictated by your financial needs?

If you make $500K a year but need every dollar of it just to keep up with your lifestyle, you're not wealthy — you're expensive.

But if you make $60K a year and you own real estate, have passive income from dividend stocks, and you're debt-free with years of savings stacked — you are wealthy by every definition that matters.

Wealth Is Taught in Silence

Here's what I learned when I got around high-net-worth individuals:

They talk about money differently.

They don't just talk about what they make. They talk about:

- Asset protection
- Tax strategy
- Passive income
- Opportunity cost
- Intergenerational transfers
- Risk-managed growth

The wealthy don't play checkers with their money. They play chess.

And the reason it all sounds foreign to so many people is because it was never spoken around them.

This is what I call the silent classroom — where the most valuable financial lessons are passed down at dinner tables, inside boardrooms, or during private conversations.

And if you weren't born into that room, you were never given the answers to the test.

Breaking the Silence: My Wealth Re-Education

Even with the financial safety net I was born into, I realized I didn't fully understand how wealth worked. I knew how to live comfortably — but not necessarily how to build independently.

That realization lit a fire in me.

I became a student of:

- Economic cycles
- Market behavior
- Private equity and real estate
- Venture capital and conservative investments
- Tax-advantaged growth and wealth transfer planning

Not because I needed to survive — but because I refused to coast. Because I wanted to create something with my fingerprints on it, not just my family name.

And what I learned changed everything.

Why You Weren't Taught This

Let's say it plain:

- Wealth is power.
- Ownership is power.
- Financial literacy is power.

So it shouldn't surprise anyone that these things have been gatekept — historically, racially, socially, and systemically.

The working class was never meant to understand capital gains.

The poor were never supposed to learn about trusts and foundations.

The incarcerated were never supposed to open brokerage accounts.

And the middle class was trained to fear "risk" while the wealthy built empires with it.

But here's the secret they don't want told:

> Once you learn how money works, you can't unlearn it.
>
> And once you start building wealth, you stop being owned.

What They Should Have Taught You

Here's the financial education I wish was required in every high school:

1. The Rule of 72 – How to estimate how long it takes your money to double.
2. Cash Flow vs. Net Worth – Understanding movement vs. magnitude.
3. Time Value of Money – Why $1 today is worth more than $1 tomorrow.
4. Good Debt vs. Bad Debt – Using leverage without becoming a slave.
5. Asset Allocation – How to spread risk without spreading yourself thin.
6. Index Funds and ETFs – The quiet engine of long-term growth.
7. The Importance of Financial Identity – How your beliefs shape your outcomes.

If you don't know these, you're not "dumb" — you're untaught. And that changes today.

Faith and Wealth: No Conflict

Let's take a moment to speak directly to the faith-minded reader:

Wealth isn't ungodly. Ignorance is. Waste is. Fear is.

God entrusted talents in the parable — and expected them to be multiplied, not buried.

The Proverbs woman invests in vineyards.

The men of wisdom leave inheritances for their children's children.

Wealth, when built with character, becomes a weapon against injustice. A platform for generosity. A legacy beyond your lifespan.

So if you've been taught that wealth is evil, let me lovingly tell you:

It's time to renew your mind.

Let's Be Honest: You're Playing Catch-Up

If you weren't taught wealth principles early on, you're playing catch-up. But that doesn't mean you've lost.

It means you'll just have to be more intentional, more focused, and more strategic from this point forward.

We don't have time for laziness. For indecision. For one-foot-in, one-foot-out thinking.

The world doesn't wait. Neither should your money.

Now You Know. Now You Move.

You've now seen the game. The veil is lifted. You understand that what you weren't taught wasn't an accident — it was by design.

But from here forward, ignorance is no longer an excuse.

You know what wealth is.

You know that you weren't taught it on purpose.

And you know that with the right mindset and action plan, you can flip the script.

Your Move

I want you to write this down somewhere:

"I was never meant to stay where I started."

That's your truth. That's your power. That's your permission.

We're just getting started. In the next chapter, I'm going to show you how to build a solid financial foundation — budgeting, saving, protecting your money — so you're not just learning to invest, but learning to keep what you earn.

Because wealth isn't built on good intentions.

It's built on strong foundations.

Let's dig in.

Chapter 3: Building a Financial Foundation – Budget, Save, Repeat

I. The Bedrock of Wealth: Why Foundations Matter

You can't build a skyscraper on sand.

That's not just a proverb — it's financial truth. Yet every day, people try to build financial futures on shaky ground. They skip the foundation, chase the dream, and when the ground shifts — a layoff, a hospital bill, a blown transmission — everything crashes down.

Let me be blunt: If you don't master budgeting and saving, you're not ready to invest. I don't care how many stock tips you hear on YouTube or what hot crypto your cousin's barber recommends. Without a solid financial foundation, you're gambling. Not investing.

I've sat in rooms with millionaires who are one lawsuit away from losing everything. I've met broke teachers who could retire early because of how faithfully they managed their income. Wealth isn't about how much you earn — it's about how well you manage what you keep.

Now let me get personal.

I was born into wealth — and I had access to resources that most people only read about. But I made a decision early: I wouldn't live off my trust fund. I'd build my own financial foundation. Not because I had to, but because I refused to be someone else's dependent — even if that "someone" was my own family.

And that foundation? It started with the basics: budgeting, saving, and building habits that honored discipline more than comfort.

Let's build yours.

II. Budget Like a Boss (Without Feeling Broke)

Most people treat budgeting like dieting — restrictive, joyless, something they only do when their life is falling apart. That mindset is the problem.

Budgeting isn't punishment. It's permission.

It gives you the power to decide what matters, where your money flows, and how your future gets built.

Think of your budget like a personal mission statement. It's your financial "yes" to the life you're designing — and your loud "no" to everything that doesn't align.

Budgeting Models: Choose Your Weapon

There's no one-size-fits-all. I've used different models at different stages of my life. You'll need to find the rhythm that works for you. Here are three proven options:

1. The 50/30/20 Model

- 50% Needs (rent, utilities, groceries)
- 30% Wants (entertainment, dining out, hobbies)
- 20% Savings & Debt Payoff

Good for: Beginners who want a clean system with clear priorities.

2. The Zero-Based Budget

Every dollar has a name. Income minus expenses equals zero. No "extra" money floating around.

Good for: People with irregular income or those recovering from debt.

3. The Real Money Method (Cash Flow Buckets)

Assign real categories: Rent, Food, Transportation, Insurance, Giving, etc. You track actuals weekly and adjust as needed.

Good for: Entrepreneurs, side hustlers, or high-income earners managing multiple streams.

Sample Budget Table (Monthly Take-Home: $3,500)

Category	Amount	Percentage
Rent/Mortgage	$1,200	34%
Utilities	$200	6%
Groceries	$400	11%
Transportation	$300	9%
Insurance	$250	7%
Savings	$500	14%
Debt Repayment	$300	9%
Entertainment	$200	6%
Giving	$150	4%

Find Your Financial Identity

There are 3 types of money managers:

- Builders – long-term, strategic thinkers who tell money where to go.
- Spenders – emotionally driven, reward-focused, and often reactive.
- Drifters – unaware of where money's going, always surprised when it's gone.

You have to know who you are before you can change how you budget.

III. The Saving Game: Not Just for Rainy

Days

Let me tell you something few will admit:

Saving is harder than investing.

Investing feels exciting — it moves, it grows, it multiplies. But saving? That's slow. Quiet. Often unrewarded in the short term. Which is why most people never do it long enough to benefit from it.

But the truth? Saving is where wealth begins.

Three-Tiered Saving Strategy

1. Short Term: Emergency Fund (3–6 months expenses)

For: car repairs, job loss, health emergencies
Where: High-yield savings account or money market account

1. Mid-Term: Opportunity Fund

For: down payment on real estate, business startup, investment opportunities

Where: CD ladders, short-term bonds, or separate savings account

1. Long-Term: Legacy Fund

For: wealth transfers, college for your kids, family trust capital

Where: long-term investments with tax efficiency (Roth IRA, 529, trusts)

Why Most People Save Wrong

- They save what's left — instead of saving first
- They keep it in checking, where it gets spent
- They don't separate savings types, so all goals blur

Let me show you how I fixed that in my own life: I automated every transfer. The moment income hits, it's split into buckets — just like a tithe. No temptation. No decision fatigue. Just discipline.

IV. Biblical Blueprint: Joseph's 7-Year Plan Still Works

Remember Joseph? Pharaoh's dream? Seven years of plenty, seven years of famine?

Joseph didn't wait for the famine to start building.

He stored up during surplus — not because he feared lack, but because he understood stewardship.

> "Let them collect all the food of these good years that are coming and store up the grain... to be held in reserve for the country, to be used during the seven years of famine." – Genesis 41:34–36

This isn't ancient history — it's economic wisdom.

In my own life, I've had seasons of massive increase. I didn't spend like a rockstar. I built like Joseph. I created buffers. I pre-funded my own setbacks. And when storms came — as they always do — I didn't flinch.

You don't save because you're afraid. You save because you're wise.

V. Budget–Save–Repeat: The Rhythmic Discipline of Wealth

This isn't a one-time thing. It's a rhythm.

Like working out, tithing, or prayer — the real power comes in repetition, not emotion.

5 Unbreakable Habits to Build

1. Automate Everything

If you have to decide to save every month, you'll talk yourself out of it. Make it invisible.

1. Review Monthly, Not Yearly

Wealth isn't built on annual reviews. It's built on monthly obedience.

1. Celebrate Savings Milestones

$1K? Celebrate. $10K? Celebrate. $100K? Take a picture and thank God.

1. Let Your Budget Flex With Life

New baby? Job change? Move? Adjust your budget like a GPS — not a grave.

1. Stay Broke While You Build

I know that sounds wild, but hear me out. Some of the wealthiest people I know live like they're broke on purpose — so they can build without pressure.

What Happens When You Get It Right?

- You stop living paycheck to paycheck
- You start sleeping better
- You begin to invest from a place of peace, not panic
- You create margin — and margin creates miracles

Most importantly, you're not just another statistic hoping for Social Security and miracles. You become a financial leader, not a survivor.

My Early Mistakes (So You Don't Repeat Them)

I used to think I didn't need a budget because I had "enough." But I was leaking wealth through undisciplined habits. I wasn't tracking spending, I wasn't separating opportunity capital, and I was ignoring the small things that become big losses over time.

What changed everything?

I began treating my finances like a business. Every dollar became an employee. Every expense, an investment or a liability. Every decision, a vote for my future self.

Final Word: Before We Start Investing...

This chapter wasn't sexy. It wasn't about stocks, crypto, or million-dollar portfolios.

But it was essential. Because every tower of wealth is only as stable as its foundation. And today — if you followed along — you just poured concrete.

From here, everything changes.

Because budgeting is power.

Saving is strategy.

And discipline? That's the new luxury.

Your Action Plan

1. Choose your budgeting method
2. Automate your savings into at least 2 buckets
3. Create your own Joseph Plan (7-month or 1-year strategy)
4. Track your money weekly — not just your balance, but your behavior

Write this on your mirror if you have to:

> "Budget. Save. Repeat. Until freedom becomes your default."

You're ready now. Let's build your investment plan next.

Chapter 4: Breaking the Chains – Escaping Poverty Mentality

> "Poverty doesn't start in your wallet — it starts in your mind. You could hand a million dollars to a man who thinks like he's broke, and in a year, he'll be broke again. But give a thousand dollars to someone who thinks like an investor? Watch what happens."

We need to talk about the part of wealth that gets ignored in most financial books — the part that has nothing to do with bank accounts, investment returns, or economic models.

This is about mindset. Mentality. Your internal blueprint.

And if we don't confront it, you'll learn everything in this book, you'll earn more than you ever imagined — and you'll still find yourself broke, stuck, or self-sabotaging.

Because the poverty mindset isn't just about lack of money.

It's about:

- Lack of vision
- Fear of abundance
- Internalized scarcity
- Deeply embedded self-doubt

And for many of us — myself included — it wasn't money we had to master.

It was the belief that we were even allowed to have it.

I. The Inheritance of Lack

I wasn't raised in poverty — I was raised in wealth. But don't get it twisted: the poverty mentality isn't limited to your environment. It's in the language you hear. The way money is treated. The assumptions you're handed before you ever touch your first dollar.

I've sat across the table from multimillionaires who still operated out of fear — fear of losing it all, fear of being exposed, fear of never "being enough."

And I've met people in prison who had almost nothing — but thought like empire-builders.

So no, this isn't about your zip code or your childhood income.

This is about what you were conditioned to believe.

If you grew up hearing:

- "We can't afford that."
- "Money doesn't grow on trees."
- "People like us just have to get by."
- "Don't be greedy."
- "That's for rich folks — not us."

...then those aren't just words.

They're chains.

II. The Symptoms of a Poverty Mentality

You don't have to be broke to think broke.

Here are the warning signs:

1. Survivor's Thinking

Living one crisis away from collapse. Always reacting. No room to dream, only hustle to make it to next week.

2. Guilt Around Prosperity

You feel bad for wanting more. You shrink when you succeed. You apologize for blessings.

3. Quick Money Obsession

Get-rich-quick schemes. Fear of long-term investing. Chasing hype over discipline. Financial ADHD.

4. Financial Blame Game

It's always someone else's fault — the boss, the system, the economy, the spouse. Never you. Never your decisions.

5. Scarcity Scar Tissue

Even when you have enough, you feel like it's not enough. So you hoard. Or overspend. Or self-sabotage.

> "As a man thinks in his heart, so is he." – Proverbs 23:7

The mind is the battleground.

III. Rewriting the Script: From Scarcity to Strategy

You don't beat poverty with money.

You beat it with renewed thinking.

Here's how:

1. Shift from Ownership to Stewardship

You don't "own" money — you manage it. God is the Source. You're the strategy.

This removes fear. You can't lose what's not yours. You're entrusted with it, not enslaved to it.

2. Trade Emergency for Legacy

Stop thinking "How do I survive this month?" and start asking "What am I building for the next 30 years?"

Poverty thinking is urgent. Wealth thinking is intentional.

3. Normalize Abundance

Speak it. Think it. Visualize it.

Start saying:

- "I always have enough."
- "Money comes to me for good use."
- "I multiply what I manage."
- "I invest in alignment, not anxiety."

These aren't affirmations — they're replacements for generational scripts that no longer serve you.

4. Honor Small Beginnings

Wealthy minds don't despise $5 saved. They understand seeds.

If you can't manage $50, you're not ready for $5,000.

Start where you are. Build discipline, not dependence.

5. Redefine What's "Normal"

For some people, being broke is normal. Struggle is normal. Drama around payday is normal. Debt is normal.

But in this book, we're redefining normal:

- Normal is margin
- Normal is sleeping well
- Normal is investing consistently
- Normal is not flinching at an emergency expense

IV. A Faith-Based Breakthrough: God Isn't Scarce

Too many believers talk about a limitless God and then live like He's bankrupt.

God is not intimidated by your goals. He's not worried about your dreams.

In fact, He's the one who put the seed of vision in you to begin with.

The problem isn't that we want too much — it's that we settle for too little.

> "I came that they may have life and have it more abundantly." – John 10:10

Abundance isn't a sin.

Lack isn't holy.

And struggle is not your birthright.

What honors God? Discipline. Wisdom. Strategy. Generosity. Ownership.

V. How I Broke the Chains Personally

Even with wealth around me, I had to break free from fear of failure, fear of comparison, and fear of letting people down.

It took:

- Budgeting aggressively even when I didn't have to
- Saying "no" to comfort so I could say "yes" to growth
- Learning to invest in my lane, not chasing other people's wins
- Trusting that God wasn't just blessing my bank account — He was maturing me

I stopped trying to look successful.
And I became it — quietly, privately, with precision.

VI. Exercises to Break Poverty Thinking

Let's get tactical.

1. Rewrite Your Money Story

Write out the 5 most common money phrases you heard growing up.

Now cross them out. Write your new money truths beneath them.

2. Set an Abundance Trigger

Pick a moment in your day — brushing your teeth, taking a shower, making coffee.

Every time you do that thing, say out loud:

> "I manage wealth with excellence and intention. I lack nothing. I'm built to multiply."

3. Audit Your Circle

Look around. Who are your top 5 voices?
Do they speak growth or fear?

Are they leveling up or spiraling down?

If you want wealth, proximity matters.

4. Stop Saying "I Can't Afford It"

Start saying:

"How can I afford it?"

"Is this aligned with my goals?"

"What do I need to shift to make this happen?"

Language shapes possibility.

VII. The Danger of Holding On to Chains

Some people are afraid of breaking the poverty mindset because poverty gave them identity. Struggle was their badge of honor. Lack made them feel humble.

But you weren't meant to wear chains just because you were born in a cage.

If you're going to step into investing, building, and legacy-making — you've got to bury the poverty script.

It's not who you are. It never was.

Final Word: You're Not Behind — You're Breaking Through

It doesn't matter how long you've thought like a struggler.

The moment you choose new thoughts, new patterns begin.

And new patterns? That's where wealth is born.

> "Do not conform to the pattern of this world, but be transformed by the renewing of your mind." – Romans 12:2

Let your mind catch up with the life you're building.

Your Breakthrough Plan

1. Identify poverty scripts in your thinking
2. Replace them with abundant truth
3. Speak new financial identity daily
4. Surround yourself with wealth-minded people
5. Practice disciplined, strategic action — even if it's small

Because this chapter isn't about theory — it's about freedom.

And real freedom? Always starts in the mind.

Chapter 5: Risk and Reward – Learning to Think Like an Investor

> "Faith and fear are both belief systems — but only one builds wealth."

If you're reading this chapter, it means you've started breaking mental chains. You've chosen to shift from consumer to investor, from surviving to building. But now comes a decision that separates thinkers from doers, and dreamers from builders.

That decision is how you handle risk.

Every investor — from Warren Buffett to the woman buying her first ETF — must understand one reality:

> No reward comes without risk.

> But not all risk is created equal. And not all fear is wise.

This chapter will show you how to:

- Think like an investor, not a gambler
- Evaluate risk with clarity and strategy
- Match your personal tolerance with financial intelligence
- Understand how the wealthy control risk instead of avoiding it
- Move from fear-based avoidance to faith-based stewardship

Let's get to it.

I. What Is Risk — Really?

Risk is exposure to uncertainty.

It's the possibility that what you put in — time, money, energy — might not produce the result you expected.

But here's the catch:

> Risk doesn't always mean danger. Sometimes, it's the door to destiny.

We're taught to fear risk. From school to work to relationships, we're conditioned to think safe is smart. But in the world of investing, playing it too safe is the fastest way to stay poor.

Let me be clear:

- No investment is guaranteed.
- But avoiding all risk is guaranteed failure.

If you hide your money under the mattress, inflation eats it. If you never step into opportunity, time will rob you. If you bury your talents — like the third servant in Matthew 25 — all you'll have to show is what you were given.

> "To whom much is given, much is required." – Luke 12:48

> And what's required? Wisdom. Courage. Calculated risk.

II. Risk vs. Reward: The Dance of Wealth

There's a principle you must memorize as an investor:

> The higher the potential reward, the higher the risk.
>
> And the lower the risk, the lower the reward.

Think of it like this:

Investment Type	Risk Level	Reward Potential
Savings Account	Low	Very Low
Treasury Bonds	Low	Low
Mutual Funds	Medium	Medium
Real Estate	Medium	Medium–High
Stocks	Medium–High	High
Startups/Crypto	High	Very High

You're not avoiding risk — you're choosing what type of risk you're willing to live with and how long you can ride it out.

III. Types of Risk You'll Face as an Investor

Let's break down the categories:

1. Market Risk

The risk that the overall market will drop — even if your specific investment is strong. Think 2008, 2020, or 2022.

2. Inflation Risk

The risk that your money loses value over time. A silent killer for people who hoard cash.

3. Interest Rate Risk

Changes in interest rates affect bond prices, mortgages, and business credit.

4. Liquidity Risk

Can you get your money out when you need it? Real estate is powerful — but not liquid. Stocks are liquid — but volatile.

5. Emotional Risk

The most dangerous of all. Your fear, impatience, and comparison can ruin a perfectly sound investment.

If you want to build real wealth, you must manage risk — not run from it.

IV. Investor Psychology: Why Most People Stay Broke

It's not just what you invest in — it's what you believe while you're investing.

Here are three emotional traps that keep people stuck:

1. Fear of Loss

Also called "loss aversion." Studies show most people feel the pain of losing $100 twice as strongly as the joy of gaining it.

This causes people to:

- Pull out too early
- Avoid stocks altogether
- Miss the rebound after a downturn

2. The Herd Mentality

When everyone's buying crypto, you do too. When everyone panics and sells, you follow. This mindset creates bubbles and crashes.

Smart investors stay calm. They buy when others panic. They sell when others get greedy.

3. Instant Gratification

If you're not okay with delayed reward, you'll never win at investing. You'll chase hype, fall for scams, and miss the slow-building power of compound interest.

V. My Story: When I Took the Right Risk

Let me tell you about a property deal I almost passed on.

It was an undervalued multi-family unit in a neighborhood that most investors overlooked. It needed work. The numbers weren't flashy. It required patience.

But I saw potential. The fundamentals were solid. The city had approved new zoning. And I knew the area.

Most of my advisors said, "Too risky."

But I said, "It's a managed risk."

I bought it.

Three years later, the area exploded. Rents doubled. Property value tripled. And I didn't just win financially — I helped revive a community.

That's the power of understanding your lane, evaluating the real risk, and trusting wisdom over emotion.

VI. Risk-Tolerance: What Type of Investor Are You?

Not everyone has the same stomach for risk — and that's okay. You need to know yourself before you invest.

Here's a simple way to self-assess:

Conservative

- You lose sleep over market dips
- You prefer safety over returns
- Ideal for: Bonds, CDs, dividend stocks, real estate trusts

Moderate

- You're okay with short-term losses if long-term gain is likely
- You value diversification
- Ideal for: Mutual funds, balanced portfolios, real estate

Aggressive

- You accept volatility in exchange for higher growth
- You love opportunity and can handle downturns
- Ideal for: Individual stocks, growth ETFs, crypto (cautiously), startups

Note: Your risk tolerance can change over time. When you're young, you can take bigger swings. As you get closer to retirement, preservation becomes priority.

VII. Risk Is Biblical — So Is Reward

Let's take it back to the parable of the talents in Matthew 25.

Three servants. Three amounts of money. Two invested. One buried it.

Guess who got praised?

> *"Well done, good and faithful servant... You have been faithful over a little; I will set you over much."*
> *– Matthew 25:21*

The one who buried it — out of fear — was rebuked.

Why?

Because he avoided risk in the name of safety — and produced nothing.

God doesn't bless hoarding. He blesses wise stewardship.

When you invest with integrity, strategy, and faith — that is worship.

VIII. Practical Tools for Managing Risk

Let's get tactical. Here's how you can take calculated risks without being reckless:

1. Diversify

Never put all your money in one stock, one asset class, or one business. Spread it.

2. Dollar-Cost Average

Invest consistently over time, instead of trying to "time the market."

3. Know Your Exit Plan

Always ask: "What's my goal, and when will I sell?"

4. Keep Cash Reserves

Never invest money you'll need in the next 12–24 months.

5. Use Long-Term Strategy

Let compounding do the heavy lifting. Time is your secret weapon.

IX. When NOT to Take Risk

Not all risk is holy.

Avoid these traps:

- Investing to impress someone
- Risking money you can't afford to lose
- Taking financial advice from people with no fruit
- Borrowing to invest without a real strategy
- Letting FOMO (fear of missing out) override facts

Faith takes action — not desperation.

X. Final Word: Move with Wisdom and Courage

Let me say it like this:

If you're not willing to risk, you're not ready to grow.

But if you risk without wisdom, you'll drown in regret.

This chapter isn't about jumping headfirst into stocks or Bitcoin.

It's about thinking like an investor — someone who:

- Studies before spending
- Plans before purchasing
- Prays before panicking
- Moves in alignment, not anxiety

God is not calling you to be reckless.

He's calling you to be ready.

And readiness looks like education, strategy, and faith-filled action.

Your Next Steps

1. Determine your risk tolerance
2. Start tracking your emotional triggers around money
3. Build a basic diversified investment plan
4. Read one book or watch one real investor interview per week
5. Invest a small, consistent amount monthly — even if it's just $50

CHAPTER 6: UNDERSTANDING STOCKS – THE LANGUAGE OF OWNERSHIP

◈ Tex Talks: If you don't understand stocks, you don't understand wealth.

Stocks aren't just ticker symbols—they're ownership. That means when you buy in, you ain't just watching from the bleachers... you're stepping onto the field. Let's break it down.

I. STOCKS ARE OWNERSHIP—NOT LOTTERY TICKETS

Before anything else, let's set the record straight: stocks are not toys, and the stock market is not your personal casino. This isn't Vegas. This isn't Lotto. This is ownership. That's the power of a stock—it makes you an equity holder in a real business. That means when a company profits, you benefit. When it crashes, you bleed with it.

When I invest in a company like Coca-Cola, I'm not buying soda—I'm buying global distribution, bottling rights, contracts, trademarks, vending machine real estate, and market share in over 200 countries. I'm buying every employee's effort and every boardroom decision. That's ownership, not luck.

Ownership gives you access to wealth creation, not speculation. The problem is, too many people treat stocks like Powerball tickets—hoping to hit a homerun instead of building something sustainable. But hope is not a strategy. In the real world, investing requires study, timing, discipline, and respect for the game.

II. TWO FLAVORS: COMMON AND PREFERRED STOCK

Stock comes in two primary varieties: common stock and preferred stock. Both represent ownership, but they function differently.

Common stockholders get voting rights, the possibility of dividends, and they participate in capital appreciation. They're at the heart of every shareholder meeting and feel every bump in the road. Preferred stockholders, on the other hand, usually don't get a vote, but they get their money first if things go south. They also enjoy steady dividends that are more like bond payments than wild rides.

Picture it like this: common shareholders are the day-to-day riders in the rodeo—they live and breathe the action. Preferred shareholders are more like box seat ticket holders—they're above the dust and chaos but don't influence the show.

In most cases, retail investors like you and me are dealing with common stock, and that's just fine—because it offers the greatest potential upside when the company grows.

III. HOW STOCKS ARE TRADED:

EXCHANGES AND MARKETS

Stocks trade in organized environments called exchanges. These are high-tech platforms that connect buyers and sellers. The two main exchanges in the United States are the New York Stock Exchange (NYSE) and the NASDAQ.

The NYSE is where older, well-established companies tend to list—companies with strong earnings and long-term track records. Think of Coca-Cola, McDonald's, JPMorgan Chase. The NASDAQ, on the other hand, is home to most of the tech world—companies like Apple, Amazon, Google, and Tesla.

Then there's the OTC market, or over-the-counter—a place where lower-quality or unlisted stocks trade. It's less regulated and more volatile. You can make money there, sure—but you can also get burned. These are the backroom deals of the stock world. Be smart, be cautious, and never invest blindly in a stock just because it's cheap.

> ◈ Tex Talks: Cheap doesn't mean valuable. OTC is where confidence goes to die.

Almost all trading today is electronic. The days of frantic floor traders screaming "Buy! Sell!" are mostly gone—replaced by algorithms, mobile apps, and 5G execution speeds. But don't get it twisted: when you press buy, you're making a business decision. Not a swipe. Not a wish.

IV. HOW STOCKS MAKE YOU MONEY

Stocks make you money through capital appreciation, dividends, and stock buybacks.

1. Capital Appreciation

This is when you buy low and sell high. For example, if you bought Netflix at $90 and sold it at $300, you just made a profit of $210 per share. But price gains are never guaranteed. That's why you study earnings, management, industry trends, and economic factors.

2. Dividends

Some companies pay out a portion of their profits directly to shareholders, typically quarterly. These payments are called dividends, and they offer passive income—even if the stock itself doesn't go up.

If you own 100 shares of PepsiCo and they pay $1.15 per share per year, you're pocketing $115 a year just to hold the stock. Reinvest that dividend and you're compounding your return over time.

> ◈ Tex Talks: Dividends are rent checks from tenants you never have to evict.

3. Stock Buybacks

When a company buys back its own stock, it reduces the number of shares available. This typically makes each remaining share more valuable. It's also a bullish sign that leadership believes the stock is undervalued.

When Apple buys back billions in stock, it's not just cleaning up the cap table—it's giving you a bigger slice of the pie.

V. BLUE CHIPS VS. PENNY STOCKS VS. GROWTH STOCKS

There are three types of stocks every investor should understand:

Blue-Chip Stocks

These are household names: companies with strong balance sheets, global reach, and decades of performance. They usually pay dividends and don't fluctuate wildly. Think Procter & Gamble, Johnson & Johnson, Coca-Cola.

They're the tortoises—slow and steady wins the wealth race.

Growth Stocks

These companies are reinvesting profits for expansion. They often don't pay dividends because they need that cash to grow. Think Shopify, Roku, or Palantir. You're buying potential, not stability.

Great if you're young, patient, and educated.

Penny Stocks

Anything under $5/share. Often unprofitable, unregulated, and unloved. They can pop 200% in a day—or go to zero overnight. High risk, low visibility.

> ◈ Tex Talks: Blue chips build portfolios. Growth stocks build momentum. Penny stocks build graves. Know the difference.

VI. READING A STOCK QUOTE

Reading a stock quote is like reading the vitals on a patient—it tells you how healthy your investment really is.

Let's break it down:

- Symbol: AAPL (Apple Inc.)
- Price: $192.75 — last trade price
- 52-Week Range: $144.25 – $199.62 — lowest/highest price over the year
- Volume: 74,000,000 — how many shares traded today
- Market Cap: $3 Trillion — value of all outstanding shares
- PE Ratio: 31.2 — price-to-earnings ratio (valuation)
- Dividend Yield: 0.5% — annual return from dividends

If the PE Ratio is high, that may mean investors expect future growth—or that the stock is overvalued. If the

Dividend Yield is high, it may signal good income—or trouble if the price dropped.

> ⟐ Tex Talks: You don't have to be a math wizard—but if you can't read a stock quote, you're flying blind. Learn the dashboard before you drive the car.

VII. THE PSYCHOLOGY OF STOCK OWNERSHIP

Stock ownership does something to your brain.

You stop seeing the world as a consumer and start seeing it as an investor. Suddenly, every store you walk into, every app you open, every product you buy is a business case.

You drink Starbucks? Cool. But now you care about traffic flow, seasonal menu changes, and loyalty app adoption. You watch Disney+? Then you'd better be listening to their next earnings call to track subscriber growth.

Owning stocks wires you for long-term thinking. It breaks the habit of emotional spending and replaces it with strategic investing. The mindset shift alone is worth the buy-in.

> ⟐ Tex Talks: When you think like an owner, you spend like a strategist. That's the first step toward sovereignty.

VIII. STARTING YOUR STOCK JOURNEY

You've got the knowledge. Now here's how to apply it:

1. Open a Brokerage Account

Fidelity. Charles Schwab. Robinhood. Webull. Take your pick. Make sure it's safe, regulated, and offers educational tools.

2. Fund It

Even $100 is enough to get started. Don't wait until you "have more money." Start with what you've got, and scale up as you learn.

3. Pick a Company You Know

Look around your life. Where do you spend money? Walmart, Target, Netflix, Nike—start there. Research them. Learn their story. Read their earnings.

4. Buy Your First Share

It's not about getting rich on the first try. It's about starting your investor journey. Once you own even one share, your brain rewires itself. You'll never look at money the same way again.

5. Track It

Watch the stock. Follow the news. Set alerts. Read quarterly reports. Become a student of the market.

> ⯑ Tex Talks: You don't need millions to start. You need movement. Start where you are, with what you have, and learn like your future depends on it—because it does.

IX. FINAL WORD: STOCKS AS A TOOL FOR FREEDOM

This chapter wasn't just about shares and dividends. It was about mindset.

Owning stock means you've crossed the line—from watcher to owner, from worker to wealth builder. And no matter where you're starting from, that shift is sacred.

You understand what stocks are.

You know the different types.

You can read a stock quote.

You have a plan to begin.

Now it's up to you. Open that account. Make that trade. Begin the journey.

ACTION STEPS:

1. Open a brokerage account
2. Identify 3 companies you spend money with

3. Read their last earnings report
4. Watch 1 tutorial on reading stock charts
5. Buy your first share—no matter how small
6. Start your investment journal

◈ Tex Talks: This isn't a game. It's the first play in your wealth strategy. Welcome to the table, boss. Now build.

CHAPTER 7: RISK & REWARD — Learning to Think Like an Investor

---

◈ Tex Talks: You can't win big without the guts to lose small.

Risk is the toll you pay to cross the bridge to wealth. But smart investors don't fear it—they calculate it.

I. THE NATURE OF RISK

Risk is not the villain in the investment story—it's the test. It's the toll you pay to cross the bridge into wealth.

Most people fear risk because they misunderstand it. Risk doesn't mean you'll fail. Risk means there's a range of possible outcomes, and some of those outcomes won't favor you.

When you invest, you're choosing to step into that uncertainty armed with information, strategy, and courage. It's controlled exposure, not blind luck. Smart investors view risk as a lever: with the right knowledge, it can amplify success. Without understanding, it'll tear your portfolio—and your confidence—to shreds.

So we don't run from risk. We don't freeze.

We walk up to it, shake its hand, and make it work for us.

II. THE TYPES OF INVESTMENT RISK

There's more than one kind of risk in investing. Think of them like threats on a battlefield—some are obvious, some are hidden, and some are inside your own camp.

1. Market Risk

The entire market declines due to external shocks like war, interest rate hikes, pandemics, or economic collapse.

2. Company-Specific Risk

The stock tanks because the business itself fails—bad leadership, weak earnings, lawsuits, or corporate scandal.

3. Industry Risk

Entire sectors fall. Think of oil in the age of electric vehicles or retail in the rise of Amazon. Trends can drag down every stock in a category.

4. Liquidity Risk

You can't sell your investment quickly or at a fair price. This hits especially hard in penny stocks or microcap plays.

5. Inflation Risk

Your money grows on paper, but inflation outpaces it. You earn 4%, but inflation is 6%. You're losing silently.

6. Emotional Risk

This one's the killer. Fear, greed, ego, and FOMO (fear of missing out) drive more losses than any index ever has.

> ⟐ Tex Talks: You can hedge against the market. You can't hedge against your own lack of discipline.

III. THE RISK-RETURN TRADEOFF

The greater the potential reward, the greater the risk. That's not pessimism—it's physics. It's how the universe balances greed and gravity.

If you want a guaranteed return, you get a savings account with 1%. If you want 20% returns, you'd better be ready for blood in the water.

This tradeoff is why bonds return 2–4% while tech startups might 10X—or go to zero. There is no such thing as a high-return, no-risk investment.

> ⟐ Tex Talks: If someone offers you big upside with zero downside, walk away. That's a fairytale in a trench coat.

Ask yourself:

- Can I survive if this goes sideways?
- If it works, will it move the needle?
- Do I understand what I'm truly risking?

You're not just risking money. You're risking opportunity cost, time, emotional stability, and long-term financial positioning.

Don't just ask, "How much can I make?"

Ask, "What happens if I'm wrong?"

IV. HOW TO CALCULATE AND MANAGE RISK

Managing risk is what separates real investors from gamblers in nice shoes. Here's how to take control:

1. Time Horizon

The longer you plan to hold, the more risk you can absorb. Never put short-term cash in long-term volatility.

2. Position Sizing

Never risk more than 2–5% of your portfolio on a single position. If you have $10K, then a $300 trade shouldn't wreck you.

3. Stop Losses

Set rules in advance. "If this stock drops 15%, I'm out." This removes emotional paralysis and protects your capital.

4. Asset Allocation

Balance your portfolio between:

- Equities (growth and blue-chip)
- Bonds or fixed income (stability)
- Cash (liquidity)
- Speculative assets (calculated risk)

5. Continuous Review

Treat your portfolio like a ranch. You check the fences, feed the cattle, and fix what's broken. Same with your holdings—review regularly and rebalance smartly.

> ◈ Tex Talks: Risk becomes manageable when it becomes measurable.

V. DIVERSIFICATION VS. DIWORSIFICATION

Diversification is protection. Diworsification is chaos.

The point of diversification isn't to own everything—it's to survive anything. You want a healthy mix of:

- Sectors (Tech, Healthcare, Energy, Financials)
- Geographies (U.S., Emerging Markets, International)
- Investment styles (Value, Growth, Income)

But if you hold 37 random stocks, and you can't explain what 15 of them do? That's diworsification.

Your portfolio should have purpose.

Every holding must serve a mission: growth, income, defense, or exposure.

> ◈ Tex Talks: If you can't explain why you own it, you shouldn't. Period.

VI. EMOTIONAL RISK: FEAR, GREED, AND THE GUT CHECK

Markets don't just crash from economics. They crash because of emotion—fear, greed, ego, panic, and pride.

Here's how it usually plays out:

- The stock drops. You panic. You sell low.
- It rebounds. You chase it. You buy high.
- It dips again. You freeze. You ride it into the red.
- Rinse. Repeat. Regret.

Emotions are natural. But rules are non-negotiable.

Ask Yourself:

- Why am I buying this?
- What's my profit target?
- What's my max loss tolerance?
- What's the plan if it drops 10%? 20%?

Don't trust your gut in the heat of battle. Trust your pre-written plan.

◈ Tex Talks: You can't always beat the market, but you better damn well beat your impulses.

VII. CASE STUDIES: WINS AND LOSSES I'VE LIVED THROUGH

These stories don't come from textbooks. They come from scars and scars come with lessons.

Pfizer (PFE) in Prison

Saw dividend increase in a three-week-old Barron's issue. Bought in blind. Two years later—34% gain plus dividends.

Why it worked: Solid fundamentals. Patience. No emotion.

GoPro (GPRO)

Loved the product. Ignored the balance sheet. Hype overruled homework. Sold at 40% loss.

Lesson: Don't marry your brand. Marry your research.

Target (TGT) During Riots

Everyone sold. I saw opportunity. Bought low when the fear was loudest. Doubled my money in 18 months.

Why it worked: Contrarian conviction + strong brand fundamentals.

VIII. RISK IN REAL LIFE: THE PRISON HUSTLER, THE RANCHER, AND THE DAY TRADER

Risk is universal. It doesn't matter if you're behind bars, riding a tractor, or clicking trades in a Manhattan high-rise.

The Prison Hustler

Trades ramen, stamps, and trust. Risking violence or time in the hole. The smart ones don't just hustle—they hedge. They know who to trust, how much to front, and when to fall back.

The Rancher

Risking livestock, feed costs, droughts, and market prices. One bad freeze can kill your entire herd. But they diversify, insure, and plan for seasons.

The Day Trader

Takes on rapid volatility. Mental stamina gets tested more than charts. But they survive through prep, pattern mastery, and cold execution.

> ⍰ Tex Talks: Everyone takes risks. But not everyone respects risk. That's the line between broke and built.

IX. TEX'S RISK RULES

1. If you can't afford to lose it, don't invest it.
2. Fear is a liar. Greed is a thief. Learn to silence both.
3. Stop losses are not signs of weakness—they're shields.
4. Risk doesn't mean reckless.
5. You are always the biggest risk in your portfolio.

X. ACTION PLAN: BUILD YOUR RISK STRATEGY

Write down your goal (growth, income, stability)

Define your time horizon

Decide how much you're willing to lose on a single trade

Set your asset allocation percentages

Pick three companies and research their risk profile

Build a rules-based system—and honor it like gospel

> ⟐ Tex Talks: Risk isn't a threat. It's a test. Pass it, and the doors to wealth swing wide open.

CHAPTER 8: Building Your First Portfolio — The Big Tex Blueprint

I: Blueprint vs. Buffet — Know Thyself First

Before You Build, Know What You're Building For

Let me say this plain:

Most people lose money in the market not because they picked the wrong stock — but because they built the wrong plan.

They jumped into investing with no blueprint. No foundation. Just vibes, YouTube clips, TikTok threads, and somebody else's confidence. That's like building a skyscraper on beach sand — flashy until the first wave hits.

Before we talk diversification, before we build your portfolio — you need to meet the investor behind it: you.

You Ain't Warren Buffett — and That's a Blessing

People love to quote Buffett. "Be greedy when others are fearful..." "Buy when there's blood in the streets..." They post Berkshire Hathaway's returns like it's their own.

But here's the cold truth:

You are not Warren Buffett.

And that's a very good thing.

Warren Buffett has:

- $150 billion in insurance float
- A team of Ivy-trained analysts
- Decades of data
- Private equity access
- Zero concern about whether his trades hit this month or next decade

You? You might have:

- A prepaid debit card
- A side hustle
- A baby on the way
- A felony record, bad credit, no cosigner, and 3 roommates

That ain't a disadvantage. That's real life — and real life breeds sharper investors when the blueprint is tailored to it.

⟐ Tex Talks:

"I didn't build my portfolio in a corner office. I built it from a prison cell, a pickup truck, and a half-rotted duplex. My edge? I knew who I was and what I needed money to do for me — and I never lied about it."

Don't borrow another man's suit. It won't fit in a storm.

The Big Tex Investor Blueprint: The 3 Truths

There are three hard truths you have to reckon with before we ever touch asset classes. Think of this as your mental balance sheet.

Truth #1: What's Your Mission? (Money Is a Hammer, Not a Home)

Every dollar you invest should be building something.

So what's the mission?

- Retire your mama?
- Buy your first 10 acres?
- Fund a clean record expungement program for your city?
- Escape the 9-to-5?
- Put a daughter through college without loans?

If you don't define the mission, the market will — and I promise, the market's mission is to make you the product.

Blueprint Prompt:

Write this down and finish it:

"I am investing because I want to ________ by ________ (date). I will not stop until I do."

Post it above your desk. On your bunk wall. On your mirror. You're not chasing stocks. You're chasing freedom with a name and a date.

Truth #2: What's Your Timeline? (Patience Has a Pay Schedule)

Here's where most people get wrecked.

They invest like they've got 30 years to wait — then panic when the rent's due in 3 weeks. Time isn't just a number; it's your weapon. And if you swing it wrong, it cuts you instead of the market.

0–3 Years:

You need stability. High-yield savings, short-term CDs, cash equivalents, maybe some dividend ETFs.

Don't risk money you'll need for emergencies.

3–10 Years:

You can afford some risk. Balanced portfolios, blue-chip stocks, quality ETFs, and some sector plays.

You're building, not gambling.

10+ Years:

Here's where the heat lives. Small caps, aggressive growth, innovation sectors, international equity, alternatives.

Volatility is your ally when time is on your side.

> ⍰ Tex Talks:
>
> "Time is your compound interest cheat code. If you ain't got patience, you don't need a portfolio — you need a paycheck."

Truth #3: What's Your Risk Tolerance? (Know What You Can Stomach)

Say you've got $10,000 invested. The market crashes. Your portfolio is now worth $7,000.

Do you:

- A) Panic sell and swear off investing forever?
- B) Hold and hope?
- C) Buy more while everything's on sale?

The answer ain't about right or wrong. It's about truth. Your truth.

Too many investors build portfolios for the person they wish they were — not the person they actually are.

And when pressure hits?

They break.

Three Real Risk Profiles I've Seen in the Wild:

1. "Bobby YOLO" – The Delusional Gambler

Wants 10X returns by Friday. Hops on meme stocks and crypto pumps. Lost $4,800 on GameStop options. "I was this close, bro."

1. "Safe Sally" – The Fearful Hoarder

Keeps everything in a savings account earning 0.5%. Inflation silently robs her every day, but she feels "secure."

1. "Slow-Burn Sam" – The Calculated Builder

Dollar-cost averages into 4 ETFs and 5 blue-chip stocks. Logs in once a week. Sleeps well.

Which one are you really?

The Gut Check:

Pull up your last three financial decisions. Were they based on:

- Emotion?
- Peer pressure?
- A written plan?

That pattern is your default setting. Name it. Then adjust it.

The Incarceration Insight: Know Your Limits, Master Your Leverage

When I was locked down, I had no Robinhood app. No real-time data. Just 3-week-old issues of Barron's and a commissary cap.

But that limitation became my advantage.

I had to make investment decisions based on principles, not hype. I didn't chase trends. I built theses.

I learned that:

- A man without self-control will always lose to volatility.
- Risk isn't just numbers — it's psychological exposure.
- Discipline is your brokerage account when you don't have one.

◈ Tex Talks:

"They took my phone, my accounts, my freedom. They couldn't touch my decision-making process. Know yourself — and nobody can take your edge."

Case Study: "Too Hot, Too Soon"

There was a guy named Dre in my block. Smart. Gifted talker. Got out, inherited $30,000 from his grandmother. Jumped into day trading like he was on Wall Street.

Within 4 months? Gone. All of it.

What happened?

He didn't know himself.

- Thought he had a high risk tolerance.
- Actually had high ego, low discipline.
- Didn't journal. Didn't plan.
- Tried to flip options like burgers.

The market humbled him. And Dre didn't need charts — he needed character.

Your Blueprint Exercise: The Investor Identity Sheet

Question	**Your Answer**
My #1 financial goal is...	
I need the money by (date)...	
I can emotionally handle losing ___% without panic.	
I plan to invest ___ per month.	
My top investing fear is...	
My top investing strength is...	

Tape it to your mirror. Revisit it monthly.

Bonus Tex Rule: Know Thy Season

Some of y'all are in a gathering season. Others in a planting season. Some of you? It's your grinding season.

- If you're broke? Focus on building your first $1,000.
- If you're stable? Focus on compound growth.
- If you're flush? Focus on capital protection and legacy.

◈ Tex Talks:

"You don't build a barn in the rain. Know your weather. Know your tools. Then build what you can sustain."

Final Words Before We Lay the Bricks

A portfolio is not a pile of stocks.
It's a reflection of the person who built it.
So get honest. Get brutal. And get started.

"The investor who knows himself doesn't panic when the world does.

The investor who doesn't — is the panic."

II: The Three-Asset Rule — Core, Growth, and Optional

Welcome to the Build Phase

Now that you've gotten real with yourself in Section I — your mission, your timeline, your risk tolerance — we can start laying bricks.

But I'm not about to drown you in Wall Street acronyms or pie charts with 37 slices.

Instead, I'm giving you The Big Tex Three-Asset Rule.

Simple enough to remember in a prison bunk.

Strong enough to build real wealth in any zip code.

> ⍰ Tex Talks:
>
> "I made my first six figures with three things: a notepad, conviction, and this rule. Don't overcomplicate freedom."

The Rule: Every Smart Portfolio Has Three Types of Assets

1. Core Assets – The bedrock. They hold up when storms hit.
2. Growth Assets – The engines. They create expansion.
3. Optional Assets – The spice. High risk, high reward.

This is your framework — whether you're investing $100 or $1 million. The exact percentages will shift based on your age, goals, and risk profile. But the structure stays solid.

Let's break them down.

I. CORE ASSETS – STABILITY WITH A PURPOSE

Think of these as your financial foundation. They're not sexy, but they're the reason your portfolio doesn't collapse when the S&P sneezes.

What Counts as a Core Asset?

- Broad market ETFs (e.g., VTI, SPY, SCHB)
- Dividend-paying blue-chip stocks (e.g., Johnson & Johnson, Coca-Cola, Microsoft)
- Bonds (U.S. Treasuries, I-Bonds, municipal)
- REITs with stable income (e.g., Realty Income)
- Money market accounts or high-yield savings (for short-term portfolios)

Why You Need Core Assets:

- They absorb shocks
- They offer income
- They compound over time
- They keep you from panic-selling when your growth assets dip

◈ Tex Talks:

> "My core portfolio once saved me $87,000 in one month — while my growth plays were bleeding red, my dividend ETFs paid me to wait."

How Much to Allocate?

50–70% for most investors

Beginners: Closer to 70%

Veterans or high-risk appetites: 50% or lower

Example:

Let's say you've got $10,000 to invest.

You might allocate:

- $4,000 in VTI (total market ETF)
- $2,000 in JNJ and KO (blue-chip dividend stocks)
- $1,000 in U.S. Treasury Bonds

That's $7,000 in Core Assets — solid, stable, working for you daily.

II. GROWTH ASSETS – ACCELERATION WITHOUT ADDICTION

Growth is where the excitement begins — but it has to be earned, not chased.

This is the section where you build above inflation, beat the market (if you can), and stack returns that compound like wildfires in dry grass.

What Counts as a Growth Asset?

- Mid-cap and small-cap stocks

- Sector ETFs (Tech, Health, Consumer Discretionary)
- Emerging markets funds
- Individual growth stocks (e.g., Shopify, AMD, MercadoLibre)

What You Need to Know:

- These assets will go up and down — violently.
- Your job is not to predict the volatility. It's to survive it with your plan intact.

Growth Requires:

Research
Risk tolerance
A long enough timeline to recover from dips

⟐ Tex Talks:

"Growth assets taught me how to think. You don't guess your way to gains. You grind your way with filings, earnings calls, and cold logic."

How Much to Allocate?

20–40% of your portfolio
If you're young with time: 40%
If you're near retirement: 20% or less

Growth Portfolio Snapshot:

From that same $10,000:

- $1,000 in QQQ (Nasdaq ETF)

- $1,000 in SMH (semiconductor ETF)
- $500 in a speculative growth stock (e.g., Palantir)

That's $2,500 total in growth.
Now you're cooking with conviction.

III. OPTIONAL ASSETS – THE CONTROLLED WILD CARD

These are not necessary. They are never to be foundational. But they can be powerful when used with precision.

Optional assets are high-risk, high-reward tools. Use them wrong and you're toast. Use them right and you accelerate freedom.

What Counts as Optional?

- Crypto (Bitcoin, Ethereum — nothing else unless you're deep in the weeds)
- Options trading
- Penny stocks
- Pre-IPO private equity
- Crowdfunding real estate
- Commodities speculation (e.g., wheat, oil, gold futures)
- NFTs (still not dead — just chaotic)

Rules for Optional Assets:

1. Never more than 10% of your total portfolio.
2. Use stop-loss orders.
3. Be willing to lose it all.

If you cry when it drops 40%, you invested too much.

⯑ Tex Talks:

“I once turned $2,800 in wheat futures into $48,000 in six weeks. Then lost $10K in two days chasing copper. These tools cut both ways — only pull them when your edge is sharp.”

Optional Allocation?

0–10% only
Beginners: Skip entirely
Seasoned traders: Cap it tight and journal every move

Example:

That $10,000 portfolio might reserve:

- $1,000 in Bitcoin
- Or $500 in ETH + $500 in covered calls

Anything more than that? You're not investing — you're rolling dice.

The Prison Blueprint Version

Let's say you're locked up. No access to brokers. No mobile apps. Maybe a loved one is trading on your behalf — or maybe you're just learning until your release.

Here's how the Three-Asset Rule applies behind bars:

- Core Assets = Knowledge. Study ETF structures, sectors, historical charts.

- Growth Assets = Strategy. Learn how market cycles affect earnings and valuations.
- Optional Assets = Simulation. Journal "would-be" trades, and grade yourself on outcomes. Focus on psychology, not flash.

◈ Tex Talks:

"In the yard, we talked options trades over chess. My stop-loss was the concrete floor. If I couldn't explain the move in one sentence, I didn't make it."

Case Study: "Don't Be a Hero" — When Optional Assets Burn

A young guy named Ronnie made his first $5,000 legally after his release. Decided to "hit it big" with weekly Tesla options.

Blew the whole account in 8 trading days.

Why?

He skipped the core. Skipped the growth. Went straight for the thrill.

He didn't build. He bet. And the market doesn't care how bad you want it.

Designing Your Own Three-Asset Portfolio (Interactive Guide)

Here's your DIY portfolio builder. Use this once you've defined your risk profile.

Asset Type	**% Allocation**	**Dollar Amount (based on your capital)**	**Notes**
Core Assets	______%	$____________________	
Growth Assets	______%	$____________________	
Optional Assets	______%	$________________	

Challenge:

Build this portfolio three times:

- One as if you're 25
- One as if you're 45
- One as if you're 65

Then compare them. See how time changes everything.

Wrap-Up: Simplicity is Power

The market will try to confuse you.
Advisors will try to impress you.
Apps will try to addict you.
But wealth starts simple:

- A foundation that holds.
- A growth engine that scales.

- A wild card you control — not the other way around.

◈ Tex Talks:

"I built $700 million in AUM with three buckets and ruthless discipline. Keep it simple. Keep it sacred."

III: Choosing Your First Three Investments

The Power of Three: Why You Only Need Three to Start

Let's kill the myth right now: you don't need 37 stocks to call yourself an investor.

You don't even need ten.

You need three smart, intentional positions. That's it.

Three horses that match your timeline, your temperament, and your thesis.

◈ Tex Talks:

"If you can't manage three stocks, what makes you think you can handle thirty? Learn to drive the pickup before you jump in the semi."

I. Rule #1: Pick One Core Investment — the Backbone

Start with something that gives you confidence, consistency, and sleep-at-night peace. This is your anchor, your no-panic zone.

Strong Choices for Core:

- Total Market ETF: VTI (Vanguard Total Stock Market)
- S&P 500 ETF: SPY or IVV
- Dividend Aristocrat: JNJ, PG, KO
- US Treasury Bond ETF: BND

What to Look For:

- Long-term track record (10+ years)
- Steady or growing dividend
- Low expense ratio (if ETF)

Example:

Greg's First Core Pick: SCHD – Schwab U.S. Dividend Equity ETF

"I wanted monthly income and blue-chip exposure. SCHD gave me both."

II. Rule #2: Pick One Growth Investment — the Accelerator

This should be something with potential — not a bet, but a play with purpose. Something with a secular trend (i.e., long-term tailwind), not a headline pump.

Strong Choices for Growth:

- Tech ETF: QQQ, XLK
- Individual Stocks: AMD, Shopify, MercadoLibre
- Emerging Markets ETF: VWO
- Small-Cap Growth ETF: IWO

What to Look For:

- Top-line revenue growth (check 10-Ks)
- Expanding total addressable market (TAM)
- High reinvestment rate into R&D

Example:

Tex's Take on AMD:

"In 2016, everyone laughed at AMD. I saw Lisa Su's turnaround strategy in the financials. Bought it at $4.30. Sold half at $21. Still hold the rest."

III. Rule #3: Pick One Optional Investment — the Experiment

This is your wildcard — a controlled risk where you test your thesis, your discipline, and your emotional management.

But here's the kicker: it must have a thesis.

If you can't explain why you own it in one sentence, don't.

Ideas for Optional:

- Bitcoin or Ethereum (5% max)
- Sector bet ETF (e.g., ARKG, for genomics)

- One options trade (cash-secured put)
- Penny stock you researched thoroughly

◈ Tex Talks:

"My first optional pick wasn't even a stock — it was a January call on wheat futures. Cost me $240. Paid out $6,700. That trade taught me more than ten books."

Optional Template:
Optional Pick: ________________
Thesis (1 sentence): ____

Entry Price: $____
Exit Plan (Profit): $____
Exit Plan (Loss): $____

IV. The "Big Tex Gut Check" Before You Buy

Don't just get excited. Get real.

Ask These 5 Questions First:

1. Do I understand how this company makes money?
2. Would I still buy it if the price dropped 30% tomorrow?
3. What would make me sell this?
4. Is this money I can afford to tie up for 2–5 years?
5. What's the edge here? Do I see something others don't?

◈ Tex Talks:

"The market is a mirror. It will show you your ego, your fear, your laziness. Answer these questions honestly, and you'll start to beat it."

V. Build Your "Starter Three" Portfolio Now

Here's a template to guide your actual decision. Print it. Fill it out. Hang it over your desk, bunk, or cell door.

Investment Type	Ticker or Name	Amount ($)	Thesis	Sell Plan (Profit/Loss)
Core				
Growth				
Optional				

Action Step:

Research one candidate for each type over the next 48 hours. Write out your full thesis in under 75 words. That's your trial run.

VI. Case Study: The Three That Built a Foundation

1. Core: SCHD

Dividend ETF, low volatility, high cashflow stability. Still holds 10+ years later.

"This gave me courage during corrections."

2. Growth: Shopify (Bought at $31, Sold at $124)

Saw e-commerce explosion coming in 2016. Read their S-1 and believed.

"Everyone mocked the price-to-sales. I saw scalability."

3. Optional: Bitcoin

Bought $1,000 in BTC at $870. Sold half at $17,000. Still holds the rest.

"Didn't invest with hope. Invested with cold risk assessment."

VII. The Prison Angle: Pick Three Without a Dollar

Even if you can't trade yet, you can practice with paper and pencil.

- Core: Study SPY's performance over 10 years. What made it resilient?
- Growth: Read Tesla's old 10-Ks. How did they position for disruption?
- Optional: Track a meme stock. Watch how news moves it. Learn emotional discipline before real money is on the table.

◈ Tex Talks:

"Freedom starts in your habits — not your holdings."

VIII. Wrap-Up: Three Is More Than Enough

The market will tempt you with shiny objects.

You'll see other portfolios with 50 names, 12 sectors, and 8 currencies.

Ignore it.

Three assets, three strategies, three disciplines — that's your start.

- One builds your base.
- One accelerates your wealth.
- One tests your mettle.

That's how wealth starts — and that's how it survives.

IV: The Psychology of Your Portfolio — Holding, Selling, and Staying Sane

I. The Mind is the Market

Before the market breaks you, it will study you.

It will read your hopes in the green candles. It will smell your panic in the red. And it will wait—silent, patient—until you blink. Then it will strike.

> ⟐ Tex Talks:
>
> "You don't lose money in a downturn. You lose it in a breakdown. Of nerve, not numbers."

What separates great investors from good ones isn't IQ. It's EQ. Emotional intelligence. The ability to hold when the world shouts "sell," and to sell when greed whispers "just a little more."

II. What Holding Really Means

When you hold an investment, you're not doing nothing. You're doing the most disciplined thing an investor can do:

You're trusting your thesis.

You're saying, "I researched this. I know this company. I know my plan." And you're letting it breathe.

Self-Check:
Should I Hold?

Has my thesis changed?

Has the company's fundamentals changed?

Or has just the stock price changed?

If your thesis holds, you hold. If your thesis breaks, you sell.

III. The Art of the Exit: When to Sell

Most investors struggle not with buying, but with selling. They ride stocks down to zero or sell too early out of fear.

Here's the Big Tex Sell Discipline Playbook:

1. The Thesis Is Broken

- CEO fired for fraud?
- Product fails FDA approval?
- Massive unexpected debt?

Sell. No questions asked.

2. Price Hits Target

Before you buy, write down:
"If this hits $X, I'll take profits."
Stick to it.

3. Portfolio Rebalancing

If one position grows to 40% of your holdings, it's time to scale down and reduce risk.

◈ Tex Talks:

"Every dollar has a mission. When the mission's complete, send it home."

IV. Emotional Triggers and How to Defuse Them

Fear

- Kicks in during downturns
- Leads to panic selling
- Makes you forget your strategy

Solution:

- Pre-set stop losses
- Pre-written journal entries: "If this drops 20%, here's what I'll do..."

Greed

- Kicks in during rallies
- Makes you over-concentrate
- Leads to bag-holding

Solution:

- Scale out gradually (sell in thirds)
- Stay tethered to the financials

Impatience

- Kicks in when stocks go sideways
- Makes you jump into fads
- Destroys compounding

Solution:

- Revisit the business plan of your company
- Track your time-in-trade vs. expectations

V. Case Studies from the Edge

March 2020 – Pandemic Panic

The markets tanked 30% in weeks. My screen was a bloodbath. My gut said: Get out now.

But I had already written my plan in January. I stuck to it.

> "Sold nothing. Bought more SCHD and PFE.
>
> By August? Account was +17%.
>
> Those who sold locked in the loss.
>
> I walked through fire and collected dividends."

The GPRO Love Affair

I loved the cameras. Thought they'd take over the media world. Bought heavy at $45.

Ignored the fundamentals:

- R&D flat
- Revenue slowing
- High churn rates

Held all the way down to $11.

Lesson: Don't fall in love with a stock. Unless that stock is TKO.

Sarah's Rule of Three

A day trader mentee of mine had a rule: "Three losses in a row, step away."

In 2022, inflation volatility hit. She lost 3 trades in a row on SPY calls.

She shut her laptop, walked her dog, reset.

Came back a day later. Next trade: +$3,100.

VI. Holding in Prison: When the Data's Late

My first year down, I had no charts. No apps. Just a pencil, old Barron's, and memory.

I held Pfizer for 14 months with no price feed. Just conviction.

Sold on a phone call when a friend read me the new dividend increase.

◈ Tex Talks:

"Can you hold what you can't see? That's real conviction."

VII. Tools to Stay Sane

The 24-Hour Rule

Never buy or sell on emotion. Sleep on it.

If the thesis still holds in the morning, act.

Worst-Case Journal

Write this before every trade:

"If this goes to zero, I lose $X. I'm okay with that because..."

If you can't finish that sentence, don't enter.

Accountability Partner

Find someone who knows your goals and your ego.

Have them ask: "What's your plan? What's changed?"

If you can't answer, you shouldn't be trading.

VIII. Wrap-Up: Mind Over Market

Your worst enemy isn't inflation or interest rates.

It's your own impulses.

Hold with reason. Sell with strategy. Stay sane with structure.

The portfolio that survives the storm isn't the flashiest —

It's the one guided by a clear head and a steady hand.

V: Building Wealth While Broke: The $10 Portfolio Plan

I. Broke Ain't Broken

Let's get something straight.

Being broke is a condition. Being broken is a choice.

You can be down to your last $3.42 and still be richer in discipline, willpower, and long-term vision than a man with $3 million and no plan.

◈ Tex Talks:

"You can't build wealth if you think broke is permanent. Broke is just where you start. Mindset is where you rise."

When I walked away from my family trust fund, I had nothing but a pre-paid debit card and conviction. The bank balance didn't matter. The belief did.

And that's what this section is about: building wealth when the world says you can't.

II. Why Starting Small Is Actually Smarter

You don't need $10,000 to start. You don't even need $1,000.

In fact, when you're just starting out, starting small is an advantage:

- You make mistakes that cost $2, not $2,000
- You learn how to read 10-Ks, earnings calls, and balance sheets without the stress of "big money" fear
- You develop the habits of real investors — research, consistency, risk management

◈ Tex Talks:

> "You don't bench 315 your first day in the gym. You lift the bar. Master the motion before you add the weight."

Small portfolios force focus. Focus builds skill. Skill scales. Period.

III. The $10 Portfolio Blueprint

Let's break it down to brass tacks.

Goal: Build real wealth with just $10 a week (or less).

How: Use one of these free or low-fee platforms:

- Cash App – lets you buy fractional shares of major companies
- Robinhood – no commissions, simple interface
- Fidelity or Schwab – more tools, more research, great for when you scale up
- Manual System (for prison readers) – track paper portfolios using old Barron's issues, write trades on envelopes, simulate investment decisions

Step-by-Step:

1. Pick One Industry You Understand

Example: Fast food, retail, energy, tech, healthcare

1. Pick One Company With These Traits:
    - Consistent earnings (check their 10-K)
    - Growing dividend or revenue
    - Clear product you believe in (but not

blindly)

2. Buy $10 worth — yes, even partial shares
3. Write down why

"I bought 0.2 shares of Pepsi because I believe its diversification in snacks and beverages provides steady growth, and its dividend yield is 2.8%."

IV. The Two-Trade Discipline

Your portfolio will be stronger if it's simple.

The Rule: Never hold more than 2 stocks at a time in your first year.

Why?

- You'll actually learn what makes them move
- You'll stay mentally engaged with their performance
- You'll be able to do real research without burning out

Diversification is good — but only after you've mastered focus.

◈ Tex Talks:

"Own what you can explain. If you can't explain why you bought it in two sentences, sell it and study harder."

V. The Commissary Investor

Let me tell you about Darryl "Stacks" Matthews — a brother I mentored in Fremont.

He had $0.00 to start. No apps. No charts. Just a battered Barron's, access to EDGAR printouts, and five envelopes marked:

- "Energy"
- "Tech"
- "Food"
- "Healthcare"
- "Wildcard"

Every month he'd take $10 from his prison job (scrubbing floors in the infirmary) and simulate a purchase by writing it on the envelope. Tracked it for 36 months.

Result?

He outperformed the S&P 500 by 12%.

Not because he was a genius.

Because he was disciplined.

VI. The $10 Playbook — Monthly Growth Strategy

Here's a sample 6-month ramp-up plan for your $10 portfolio:

Month	Goal
January	Buy 1 dividend stock (partial shares ok)
February	Research its last 10-K, summarize 3 risks
March	Add 2nd company (different sector)
April	Track earnings call for both
May	Begin price journaling weekly
June	Reassess: hold, add, or replace 1 stock

Keep going. Slow and steady beats flashy and foolish.

VII. Avoiding "Broke Bro" Syndrome

You know the type. No money, but always "investing" in the next crypto coin, meme stock, or fake guru course.

Don't flex.

Don't chase hype.

Don't trade what you don't understand.

Wealth is built, not guessed.

◈ Tex Talks:

"Stop trying to get rich in a day. Try getting consistent in a decade."

VIII. Side Hustle Math — Turn Hustle Into Holdings

Let's say you flip hoodies or artwork or even Ramen spreads.

You profit $5 a week.

That's $20/month.

At $20/month, in 10 years with 10% annual growth, you'd have over $4,000.

Add discipline? Add $5 more per week? That becomes $10K–$12K.

Compounding don't care where the money came from. It just wants to work.

IX. Mental Wealth Check-In

Before you place your next trade, answer:

- Am I investing from belief or desperation?
- Am I rushing because I'm trying to prove something to others?
- Am I buying this stock because I understand it—or because it's trending?

⯑ Tex Talks:

"A broke man with a plan will always beat a rich fool with a whim."

X. Action Plan: Your First $10 Investment

Here's what I want from you:

Write your #1 investing goal

Pick your first industry

Research 1 company

Buy $10 worth

Write down your reason

Track it weekly for 30 days

Review it and reflect

Then repeat.

This is the rhythm of the wealthy. And the broke man who learns this rhythm early? He becomes unstoppable.

VI: The Emotional Investor's Toolkit: How to Stay Rational When Markets Go Crazy

"Your worst enemy isn't the market. It's you."

I. The Two Killers: Fear and Greed

Every market crash, every blown-up portfolio, every "coulda-woulda-shoulda" story?

It boils down to two things:

- Fear — selling too soon
- Greed — buying too late

◈ Tex Talks:

> "Fear makes you fold too early. Greed makes you bet the house too late. Both rob you with your permission."

March 2020. Pandemic panic.

Stocks plummeted. The media screamed. One of my traders dumped everything — blue chips, ETFs, his own dad's retirement fund. Lost half his gains in two hours. The kicker? Two weeks later, the market bounced 27%.

He didn't lose because of COVID.

He lost because of himself.

II. The Inner War — My Prison Gut Check

Let me take you inside my own head.

It's March 18, 2020. The Dow just fell 2,997 points in a day — the largest single-day point drop in history.

I'm staring at a wrinkled copy of Barron's, 13 days old. Pfizer had quietly raised its dividend. Their COVID vaccine work had started. The price hadn't budged — yet.

My commissary fund was thin. $172 and change.

My gut screamed, "Hold it. This is it."

My fear screamed louder: "What if this crashes further? What if you just threw your last funds away?"

I breathed. I prayed. Then I remembered:

> ◈ Tex Talks Rule #3:
>
> "Stops protect strategy. Panic protects nothing."

I placed a call through my attorney. Bought 1,500 shares through my outside trust.

Two years later: +34% and a 5.4% dividend gain.

III. Tools for Emotional Mastery

Let's make this practical.

Here are five tools I personally used — and teach.

1. The 24-Hour Rule

> "If it feels urgent, it's emotional."

Never buy or sell on the same day you feel the urge. Write down your reason, sleep on it.

Revisit the trade with a cold mind.

2. The Worst-Case Journal

Take a blank page. Write:

> "If this trade goes 100% against me, I lose $______. My total portfolio drops ____%. I can live with that because ________."

If you can't finish that sentence? You're not ready.

3. The Exit Plan Pledge

Before you enter a trade, write:

> "I will sell this stock if it drops below $____ or if _____ changes in the business."

That's your stop-loss. That's your compass. Don't let the market shake it.

4. Accountability Partner

Pick someone ruthless and honest. Show them your trade idea. Make them punch holes in it.

Mine was Jamal. He once looked at a biotech stock I loved and said:

"You're buying hype, not revenue. Sit down."

He saved me $14,000 that day.

5. The Red Screen Ritual

Markets bleed. Red screens happen.

Before you touch your portfolio, repeat:

> "My process protects me. Not my feelings."

> Then go for a walk, do 20 pushups, or listen to worship music. Do anything but click 'Sell' in fear.

IV. The Psychology of Holding

Here's a truth no one tells you:

Holding is harder than selling.

Why? Because holding requires conviction without applause. No one claps for patience.

But every multi-millionaire investor I've ever met had one thing in common:

> They let winners run.

They didn't bail at +8%. They held through dips. They stayed rational.

Warren Buffett held Coca-Cola for decades.

> ◈ Tex Talks:
>
> "Sell weeds, water flowers. Don't pull your best ideas just to feel productive."

V. Selling With Honor — Not Panic

There are right reasons to sell:

◈ Business changes (CEO resigns, fraud uncovered)

◈ You hit your planned target

◈ You need liquidity for another opportunity with better risk/reward

But there are wrong reasons too:

◈ "Everyone else is selling"

◈ "The chart looks scary"
◈ "I just want to feel safe"

◈ Tex Talks:

"You're not paid for being early. You're paid for being right."

VI. Real Case: The GPRO Regret

I once fell for a story stock — GoPro.

The product was dope. I used one on my ranch. I ignored the signs:

- Inventory bloat
- Marketing costs skyrocketing
- Sales flattening

I let product love override process.
Bought at $29.
Sold at $11.
Lost $74,000.
The lesson?
Love the data. Not the brand.

VII. Action Plan: Emotional Investor Audit

Answer these honestly:

1. When markets drop 10%, do I:
    - A) Panic
    - B) Hold
    - C) Buy more?
2. Do I have an exit plan for every investment?

3. Who checks my bias when I fall in love with a stock?
4. What ritual do I follow when my emotions spike?

◈ Tex Talks:

"The market is a mirror. If you're scared, it will punish you. If you're prepared, it will pay you."

VIII. Final Word

The markets will test your process. But your emotions will test your soul.

If you master them both, wealth is yours — slow, steady, and built to last.

VII: The Ownership Mentality: Stop Renting Wealth, Start Becoming It

I. Renters vs. Owners: The Mental Divide

Let's start with a truth that'll sting:

Most people rent their entire financial life.

Not just their home. They rent their time (via paycheck).

They rent their retirement (via 401(k)s they don't understand).

They rent their peace of mind (by outsourcing their financial decisions to YouTube gurus, TikTok clowns, or worse — their broke cousin Reggie).

But the wealthy?

They own.

- They own businesses.

- They own equity.
- They own decisions.

◈ Tex Talks:

"The rich don't wait for the check. They cut it. They don't ask for the seat. They build the table."

II. The Owner's Creed

To build wealth, you must believe this:

"I am not a visitor in this economy. I am a stakeholder in its outcomes."

That means:
◈ You know where your dollars go
◈ You choose what to support
◈ You learn the tools, not just follow the trends
You're not playing the market.
You're building an empire. One trade, one asset, one decision at a time.

III. The Ownership Test

Let me give you three questions that draw a line in the sand:

1. If the stock market closed for 10 years, would I still want to own what I hold?
2. If my investment dropped 40%, could I still explain why I bought it — with data, not drama?
3. If my daughter asked me what I owned and why, could I explain it simply and truthfully?

If your answer to any of those is no, you're not an owner. You're a speculator with a Wi-Fi signal.

IV. Real Talk From the Ranch

I once bought land in East Texas — 42 acres of thorns, snakes, and dead soil. No fences. No water line. Everyone told me I was insane.

But I saw it. I knew what I was building.

So I studied irrigation. I laid pipe by hand. I planted hybrid grass, rotated cattle, brought in wind turbines.

Now? That same land generates $140K/year in beef, power, and pasture lease.

> ◈ Tex Talks:
>
> "Ownership isn't sexy. It's strategy. Sweat + vision + time = wealth."

V. The Prison Portfolio Parallel

Let's go back to a man I met inside.

His name was Miguel. Serving 15 years.

Every month, he used his commissary gig to sock away $11.

He had no Robinhood. No TD Ameritrade.

But he studied balance sheets like Psalms.

He sent buy requests through a family-run custodial account.

By year 3? He held dividend-paying shares in:

- Coca-Cola
- Duke Energy

- Procter & Gamble

His monthly passive income was $92. Inside a prison.

> "They can lock my body," he told me, "but not my cash flow."

That's ownership.

VI. The Ownership Operating System

Start with these steps:

1. Track Everything You Own

Use a simple spreadsheet or journal. Know:

- Ticker
- Entry price
- Reason for purchase
- Expected return
- Exit strategy

2. Stop Following. Start Understanding.

Don't ask "Is this a good stock?"

Ask: "What's the revenue trend? What's the debt ratio? What's the moat?"

3. Set Legacy Intentions

Write:

> "I am building wealth to pass down ___________________."

Make it personal. Not theoretical.

VII. Action Plan: Flip the Switch

Do this now:

- Open your latest investment account.
- For every position, write 1 sentence:

"I own this because ______________________."

If you can't do that?
You're just renting performance.

VIII. Final Word: From Equity to Eternity

This isn't about stocks. It's about sovereignty.

The world will try to make you a financial tenant — dependent, reactive, blind.

But you, Big Tex, are building a house on rock.

You read the fine print. You own the playbook. You refuse to flinch.

◈ Tex Talks:

"Renters beg for exits. Owners build their legacy."

Turn the page. It's time to build your portfolio.
From this point on, you own this life.

VIII: The Wealth Map: Building Your Personal Asset Allocation Plan

I. Why You Need a Map

You wouldn't drive from Dallas to Denver without a GPS.

You shouldn't build wealth without a destination and a route either.

That route is called asset allocation — the intentional mix of investments based on:

- Your goals
- Your timeline
- Your tolerance for risk
- And your capacity for emotional control

◈ Tex Talks:

"Hope is not a plan. And winging it ain't wealth. You need a damn map."

II. What is Asset Allocation?

It's how you divide your money across:

- Stocks – Ownership with growth potential
- Bonds – Loans that pay you interest
- Cash/Cash Equivalents – Stability and access
- Alternatives – Real estate, commodities, private equity, crypto
- Yourself – Business ventures, education, tools

The right mix protects you when markets fall and positions you to grow when they rise.

III. Example Maps: Profiles in Allocation

Let's break it down by stages:

"The Starter"

(Ages 18–30)

- 70% Stocks (mostly ETFs, some individual)
- 10% Bonds
- 10% Cash
- 10% Self-Investment (courses, licenses, bootstrapped biz)

Goal: Growth > Stability
Note: High volatility is okay. Time is your edge.

"The Builder"
(Ages 30–45)

- 60% Stocks (mix of growth and dividend)
- 20% Bonds
- 10% Cash
- 10% Alternatives (real estate, private placements)

Goal: Balanced growth, wealth preservation
Note: You're starting to think about legacy. Diversify with purpose.

"The Closer"
(Ages 45–65)

- 40% Stocks (blue chips, dividend-heavy)
- 30% Bonds
- 20% Alternatives
- 10% Cash

Goal: Income + Risk Protection

Note: Sequence of returns risk matters now. Keep cash for downturns.

"The Sovereign"
(Post-Retirement)

- 20–30% Stocks
- 40–50% Bonds
- 20% Alternatives
- 10–20% Cash

Goal: Peace of mind + passive income

Note: You're not chasing alpha. You're protecting freedom.

IV. My Prison Map

I built a custom map in a place where most men just survive.

⟐ Tex Talks:

"Even in chains, I mapped my money."

- 40% Dividend stocks (for slow, steady passive income)
- 20% REITs (exposure to real estate, no toilets to fix)
- 15% Bonds (stable interest payments)
- 15% Cash equivalents (short-term CDs, savings)

- 10% Private investments through outside trusts

Every piece had a job. Every dollar knew its role.

Even if I didn't walk free for ten more years — my money would.

V. Tools: Build Your Wealth Map

Step 1: Define Your "Why"

> "I'm building wealth to ____________."

Step 2: Define Your Time Horizon

Short (1–3 yrs)? Medium (3–10)? Long (10+)? Retirement?

Step 3: Know Your Risk Tolerance

Write:

> "I can afford to lose ____% in a downturn without panicking."

Step 4: Choose Your Mix

Pick from the categories above based on your goals. Customize it. Don't overthink — just begin.

Step 5: Automate & Adjust Quarterly

Use auto-deposits into diversified funds. Rebalance every 3–6 months.

VI. Your First Wealth Map Worksheet

> ⟐ EXERCISE: Grab a page or open Notes.

1. My financial goal in 10 years:

   ____

2. My risk tolerance (1–10): ______
3. My current age/stage: __________
4. My preferred % allocation to stocks: ____
5. My preferred % allocation to bonds: ____
6. My preferred % allocation to cash: ____
7. My preferred % allocation to alternatives: ____
8. What I will study this month to build skill:

   ____

9. Who I will ask to review this plan with me:

   ____

VII. Final Word: You're the Architect Now

You're not a spectator in the economy anymore.

You're the architect.

Wealth doesn't come from wishing. It comes from allocating on purpose.

So draw your map.

Sharpen your pencil.

And never forget:

> ◈ Tex Talks:
>
> "The one with the clearest plan wins. The one who sticks to it becomes wealthy."

CHAPTER 9: THE POWER OF PATIENCE (How Time Builds Empires)

I: Why the Fast Money Fades—and the Slow Money Wins

There's an old ranch saying:

> "You can't rush a bull and expect butter."

Wealth? Same rules. If you want generational riches, don't chase rabbits. Grow oak trees.

I. The Get-Rich-Quick Lie

Every week, another fool posts a crypto flex on Instagram.
Every week after, another one's crying in the comments.
That's because speed is seductive. It whispers:

> "You don't need time. You just need a hack."
>
> "You don't need discipline. You just need this ONE stock."
>
> "You don't need to build. You just need to bet."

Here's the truth:
◈ Wealth hacked = Wealth cracked
◈ Wealth rushed = Wealth crushed
◈ Wealth built = Wealth kept

II. The Compound Interest Gospel

Albert Einstein (probably) called compound interest the eighth wonder of the world. Whether or not he actually said it doesn't matter. It is.

Let's break it down real:

- If you invest $5,000 a year from age 20 to age 60...
- And earn just 8% annually (average stock market return) ...
- You don't end up with $200,000...

You end up with $1.4 million.
Why?
Because your money starts earning money.
And then that money starts earning money.
And then your kids' college fund is thanking you.
It's exponential. Quiet. Relentless. And it's slow... at first.

◈ Tex Talks:

"Compound interest is like prison time. The first-year drags. The fifth flies. The tenth changes everything."

III. The Stock You Never Sold

Let me take you back.

1. I had a kid walk into Carbonado with a thousand-dollar tax refund. Didn't know stocks from sneakers. But he listened.

I pointed him to Apple (AAPL) — $14.76/share (split-adjusted).

He bought 67 shares.

Fast forward 10 years: stock price over $170.

He never sold.

Total value? Over $11,000.

Dividends reinvested. Zero stress. Zero trades. Just time.

He's now 35. A six-figure portfolio, never earned more than $60K a year. Why?

He didn't try to be brilliant.

He dared to be boring.

> ◈ Tex Talks:
>
> "The boring money becomes the freedom money."

IV. The Prison Mindset Flip

Behind bars, I learned the real value of time.

Because when you're doing a stretch...

- You start to see seasons, not seconds.
- You think in patterns, not panic.
- You feel how slow builds depth.

I watched men turn:

- Commissary hustle into college degrees
- GEDs into stock portfolios
- Bible studies into peace of mind

The ones who grew? They stopped chasing.

They planted. Then they watered. Then they waited.

Patience wasn't weakness. It was warfare.

V. The Fast Money Graveyard

Let me show you what impatience costs.

A trader named Malik came through the bootcamp. Sharp. Charismatic. Hungry.

He found a biotech stock surging on Reddit.

Didn't read the 10-K. Didn't check the burn rate.

Dropped $4,700 into it — everything he had.

Two weeks later, FDA pulled approval.

Stock cratered 93%. Game over.

I sat him down. Said:

> "You didn't invest. You gambled with your grandma's prayers."

He cried. Then he rebuilt.

Now? He's 32. Married. Real estate income. $84K in a Roth IRA.

But that lesson? It cost him.

VI. What the Wealthy Know

The rich understand one thing:

> Time is the only leverage that doesn't lie.

- Real estate magnates wait out market cycles.
- Stock market giants hold blue chips for decades.

- Entrepreneurs build companies over years—not weeks.

They don't flinch when the market dips.
They don't sell on emotion.
They let compound interest, dividends, and capital appreciation do what hustle never can.
They don't chase the money.
They let the money chase them.

VII. The 5-Year Rule

Want a filter to separate get-rich schemes from empire plays?
Ask this:

> "Would I still own this asset 5 years from now...
> even if no one else knew I had it?"

If the answer is no, don't touch it.
Because wealth isn't just built by what you buy.
It's built by what you refuse to sell.

VIII. Action Steps: Building Your Time Armor

1. Start an Investment Journal:
   Track every trade or purchase. Include:

   - The reason for buying
   - The time horizon
   - The exit plan
   - The emotional state when entering

2. Study 3 Long-Term Wealth Builders:
Look up:

- Warren Buffett (stocks)
- Barbara Corcoran (real estate)
- Robert Smith (private equity)

3. Take the 12-Month Challenge:
Pick one ETF or dividend stock.
Invest monthly.
Don't sell.
Don't check daily.
Don't flex online.
Just build. In silence. With power.

IX. Final Word: The Seed Strategy

This chapter isn't about slowness.
It's about compounding force.
Plant your seed.
Guard it.
Water it.
And walk away if needed — trust the soil.
Because the man who waits?
Owns the land.

◈ Tex Talks:

"If you're not patient with small profits, you'll never be worthy of generational ones."

II: The Math of Multiplication — Understanding Compounding Like a Millionaire

I. What Is Compounding?

Let's get straight to it: Compounding is the art of making your money reproduce.

It's not just earning on your investment — it's earning on the earnings from your investment.

It's a flywheel:

You push.

It turns.

You push again.

It spins faster.

Then — one day — it flies on its own.

⟐ Tex Talks:

"Compound interest is the closest thing we've got to legal cheating."

II. The Numbers Game

Let's walk the slow money path:

Scenario 1:

- You invest $100/month starting at age 20.
- You do it for 40 years.
- You earn just 8% a year.

You'll have over $300,000.

Now look at the flip:

Scenario 2:

- You start 10 years later — at 30.
- Same $100/month.
- Same 8% return.

Your final amount?

$140,000.

Same money.

Half the time.

Less than half the wealth.

Why?

Because the first 10 years weren't just time — they were acceleration.

That's how millionaires think: in multiples, not moments.

III. The Rule of 72

Let me bless you with a tool every real investor keeps in their back pocket:

The Rule of 72

Take 72, divide it by your expected annual return rate — that tells you how long it'll take your money to double.

So:

- At 8% return, 72 ÷ 8 = 9 years to double your money.
- At 12%, it only takes 6 years.

- At 4% (bank savings)? You're waiting 18 years.

⟐ Tex Talks:

"If your money ain't doubling, your grind is just noise."

IV. Real Wealth = Time x Rate x Discipline

Let's break that formula down:

- Time gives you scale
- Rate gives you speed
- Discipline makes sure you don't blow it up

Case Study: The Dividend Machine

- In 2014, I bought PepsiCo (PEP) for $78/share
- Reinvested dividends. Never sold.
- Today? Over $170/share, plus annual dividend growth
- That's price gain + payout growth = compounded muscle

I didn't trade it.
I didn't brag about it.
I held the line.

⟐ Tex Talks:

"Discipline turns time into treasure."

V. Compounding vs. Trading: The Reality Check

Investor A (Compounding)	**Investor B (Trader)**
Buys 5 dividend stocks	Flips meme stocks weekly
Reinvests gains	Withdraws profits (and losses)
Earns 9%/year for 20 yrs	Hits 25%... then -40%...
Ends with $470K	Ends with anxiety (and $88K)

The math doesn't lie.

The market doesn't care if you're clever — it rewards the one who waits.

VI. Micro vs. Macro: Letting Time Shrink Your Mistakes

Everyone makes a bad investment.

But here's the truth:

Bad trades lose money fast.

Great investments make money slowly — but permanently.

"I bought too early." — Time forgives that.

"I bought too small." — Time scales that.

"I bought the wrong stock." — Time replaces that, if you learn.

Macro thinking (long game) always wins over micro panic.

VII. Your Patience Multiplier Table

Monthly Investment	10 Years	20 Years	30 Years	40 Years
$25	$4,570	$14,641	$36,886	$95,103
$100	$18,280	$58,563	$147,544	$380,415
$250	$45,700	$146,408	$368,860	$951,038
$500	$91,400	$292,816	$737,720	$1.9M

(Assumes 8% average return, monthly contribution, no withdrawals.)

💭 Tex Talks:

"You don't need to be rich to build wealth. You just need to be patient on purpose."

VIII. Final Challenge: Your Compounding Covenant

Write this down. Post it on your wall. Memorize it.

"I will invest for the future me.

I will be patient with my wealth.

I will let compounding multiply what hustle alone cannot."

Then commit to:

- One automatic monthly contribution
- One dividend reinvestment decision
- One year of not checking your portfolio weekly

Because when patience becomes your weapon, compounding becomes your army.

III: What If You're Starting Late? (The Power of Catch-Up Investing)

I. No Shame in a Late Start

First things first:
Forget guilt. Forget shame. Forget regret.
If you're 35, 45, 55, or even 65 and just now learning this game — you're still in it.

◈ Tex Talks:

"Regret don't pay dividends. Action does."

Wall Street loves to scare you with youth math:

"If you didn't start at 18, you'll be broke forever!"

That's a lie.

Yes, early starters have the time advantage.
But late starters? We've got something stronger:
Urgency
Discipline
Focus
And those three? They can move mountains.

II. The 10-Year Miracle Plan

You don't need 40 years.
You need 10 with discipline.
Here's a sample breakdown for a late starter (age 45–55):

- Invest $1,000/month
- Average return: 8% annually
- 10 years of consistency

Final portfolio: $183,000+
Add 10 more years without contributing = $395,000
That's how compound interest keeps paying you — even when you stop feeding it.

III. Catch-Up Weapons You Can Use Today

1. Max Out Retirement Accounts

If you're 50+, the IRS gives you extra space:

- 401(k): Up to $30,000/year (including $7,500 catch-up)
- IRA: Up to $8,000/year (including $1,000 catch-

up)

That's over $38,000/year of tax-advantaged growth. Use it.

---

2. Use "Stacking" Strategy

Don't just set it and forget it. Stack your moves.
Example:

- Invest $1,000/month
- Reinvest dividends
- Allocate bonuses or side hustle income to lump sum buys
- Use every tax refund to purchase quality ETFs or dividend stocks

This is snowball discipline — and it rolls fast.

---

3. Leverage Time-Weighted Focus

If you're older, you don't need risky growth plays. You need:

- Dividend stocks
- Index funds
- Cash-flowing REITs
- ETFs with covered call strategies

Focus on preserving capital while growing smartly.

IV. What If You Only Have 5 Years?

Then we play defensive offense:

- Target conservative growth + guaranteed income
- Load Roth IRAs with dividend aristocrats (think PEP, JNJ, KO)
- Add short-term bond ETFs
- Consider annuities with guaranteed minimum income (get a fiduciary)

And most importantly? Cut lifestyle creep.

◈ Tex Talks:

"At 25, you can waste a dollar.

At 55, every dollar's a soldier. Deploy with strategy."

V. Real-Life Late Bloomers

Case Study: Tyrone "Trigger" Jones – Age 48

- Former street hustler turned forklift operator
- Started saving $800/month in a Roth IRA
- Bought nothing but SCHD, VTI, and utilities
- In 12 years?

$210,000

Cash-flowing over $7,000/year in dividends
Down payment on a duplex rental

Trigger's line:

"My patience outworked my past."

VI. The Power of Momentum

It's not about age.
It's about direction + momentum + belief.

- Start now
- Keep going
- Don't flinch when you plateau
- Compound discipline just like money

Because the truth is this:

Starting late with intensity beats starting early with laziness. Every time.

VII. Action Challenge: Your Catch-Up Covenant

◈ Write this out and tape it to your fridge, mirror, or bunk:

"I may have started late. But I will finish free.

Every dollar I invest is time redeemed.

I will catch up. I will stay in. I will win."

Then:

- Open your IRA today (Roth if eligible)
- Set your monthly auto-contribution
- Choose 1 long-term ETF (start with VTI or VOO)
- Ignore the noise. Compound in silence.

◈ Tex Talks:

"It's not too late — unless you believe the lie. Move now. Make it count."

IV: The Compounding Myths That Keep People Broke

I. Myth #1: "I Don't Make Enough to Invest"

Reality: You don't need a six-figure salary — you need a six-second decision.

If you can spend:

- $8 on fast food,

- $15 on lottery tickets, or
- $35 on shoes you don't need,

...then you can invest $25/month. That's $0.83 a day.

🧭 Tex Talks:

"You ain't broke — you're misaligned."

Let's break it down:

- $25/month at 8% = $36,000 in 30 years
- $100/month = over $147,000
- $250/month = nearly $370,000

Still think you're too broke to invest?

Money grows in motion, not excuses.

II. Myth #2: "It's Too Late For Me"

Reality: The only thing too late is never starting.

Late starters often:

- Make fewer mistakes
- Focus better
- Take things more seriously

One of my students, Marcus, started investing at age 53 after doing 18 years inside.

By 63?

- His IRA was worth $140,000
- He owned a paid-off duplex
- He collected $5,700/year in dividend income

He started later than most.
But he started harder than most.

◈ Tex Talks:

"Late bloomers still bloom. Ask the rose."

III. Myth #3: "Investing Is Too Complicated"

Let me say it plainly:

- If you can use Facebook, you can use an investing app.
- If you can read gossip blogs, you can read a stock's 10-K.
- If you can do prison calculus to stretch your commissary, you can compound capital.

What they call "complicated" is just deliberately intimidating.

Because if you understood how simple it was, you'd be free.

Here's how it works:

- Buy index funds or blue-chip stocks
- Reinvest dividends
- Don't sell unless the thesis breaks
- Add consistently
- Wait

That's 80% of wealth building. The other 20% is patience.

IV. Myth #4: "You Need a Financial Advisor"

No.
You need a plan, not a babysitter.
Financial advisors are fine — if they're fiduciaries.
But most are salespeople with licenses.
Here's what you do instead:

- Use Vanguard, Fidelity, or Charles Schwab
- Buy low-cost index funds (VOO, VTI, SCHD)
- Set up automatic contributions
- Check it once a quarter — not every week

No fees. No middleman. No fluff.

◈ Tex Talks:

"You don't need permission to build wealth. You just need precision."

V. Myth #5: "It's Safer to Keep Cash"

Let's put this one in a coffin:

Inflation is theft.

If inflation averages 3% and your savings earns 0.01%, you're losing money every day.

Let's break it down:

- $1,000 in a shoebox for 20 years = $1,000
- $1,000 invested at 8% = $4,660+

Your dollars are dying in the dark. Invest or watch them rot.

VI. Myth #6: "The Market Is Rigged"

No.

The game isn't rigged — but your mindset might be.

Yes, big players have an edge.

Yes, the news manipulates emotion.

Yes, there are crashes, panics, dips, and scams.
But you don't need to beat the hedge funds.
You need to beat your excuses.
Compounding doesn't care who you are.
It rewards those who stay in the game.

◈ Tex Talks:

"This game ain't fair — but it's still winnable."

VII. The One Truth: Time Is the Only Equalizer

It doesn't matter if you're:

- Black, white, brown, or broke
- In a cell or in a suit
- 18 or 58

If you give compound interest enough time, enough consistency, and enough discipline — it will work.

Time doesn't play favorites.
It pays those who play long.

VIII. Challenge: Myth-Buster Manifesto

Write this in your journal, workbook, or wall:

"I am not too broke.

I am not too late.

I am not too dumb.

I am not too far behind.

I will build wealth — slowly, steadily, and strategically.

Because time is on my side."

Then:
◈ Identify 1 myth you've believed
◈ Write out how it's cost you
◈ Replace it with 1 truth
◈ Act on that truth this week

V: The Seeds You Never See — Real Stories of Quiet Wealth Built Over Time

I. The Janitor With $8 Million

Ronald Read swept floors at a Vermont gas station. Later, he worked as a janitor at JCPenney. Wore flannel, drove a beat-up car, clipped coupons.

When he died at 92?

He left $8 million.

Half to the library. Half to the hospital.

How?

- Bought blue-chip stocks
- Reinvested dividends

- Held for decades
- Never panicked, never sold

He owned Procter & Gamble, JPMorgan, Johnson & Johnson.

> ◈ Tex Talks:
>
> "He mopped floors — and cleaned up on Wall Street."

II. The Prisoner With a Portfolio

Dallas County Jail. 2015.

Andre M., 37 years old.

Ten-year sentence. No family support. Just a GED, a Bible, and a dog-eared Barron's from 2013.

He found an old Thinkorswim login from before his arrest. Called his sister:

> "Transfer the $800 to an account under your name. I'll direct every move."

Over the next five years:

- Bought dividend stocks during earnings dips
- Read 10-Ks with a flashlight
- Called in trades once a week
- Never chased hype

By his release?

$17,000 in that account

Four positions with 4–6% annual yield

Enough to buy a used car, a laptop, and apply for housing

His first job out? Warehouse. His first side hustle? Teaching other ex-felons how to open a Roth IRA.

◈ Tex Talks:

"He lost a decade of freedom — but not a second of financial clarity."

III. The Stay-at-Home Mom Who Retired a Millionaire

Lisa B. had no formal job. Raised three kids. Clipped coupons, ran the household. Her husband made $60,000/year.

But Lisa had a secret:

She treated their budget like a business.

- Cut spending by 30%
- Invested the difference in Vanguard index funds
- Tracked dividends in a notebook
- Avoided lifestyle creep like the plague

They never looked rich.

But by 65, they had:

- $1.1 million in retirement
- A paid-off home

- A rental duplex they bought with stock dividends

Her kids joked she was "cheap."
Now they call her "CEO Mom."

◈ Tex Talks:

"She never chased wealth. She invited it, consistently."

IV. The CO Who Built Quiet Wealth Behind the Fence

Jerome L., corrections officer in Ohio. 29 years at the same facility.

He never traded. Never speculated. Never flexed.
But:

- Contributed the max to his 401(k)
- Bought shares of his prison's private contractor (CXW) during dips
- Reinvested dividends for 25 straight years

On his last day?

- Cashed out $812,000
- Had another $3,000/month in pension
- Moved to Panama

The inmates never knew.

The staff never guessed.

But every compound interest calculator would've predicted it.

◈ Tex Talks:

"Some folks shout about wealth. Others build it in silence. Be the latter."

V. What All These Stories Share

- No rich parents
- No financial degrees
- No flashy trades

Just:
◈ Patience
◈ Repetition
◈ Long-term thinking
◈ Faith in time
That's the formula. That's the flex. That's the future.

VI. Action Step: What Seed Will You Plant Today?

Grab a journal.
Write:

"I will become the quiet millionaire.

I will invest consistently, silently, and strategically.

The harvest will come. Until then, I sow with discipline."

Then:

- Open a brokerage account
- Invest in 1 dividend stock or ETF
- Commit to auto-invest monthly
- Journal your "Wealth Date" — the day you started

Because five years from now, you'll look back at this moment and realize:

This was the chapter that changed everything.

VI: Tex's Patience Playbook — Real Tools for Long-Term Wealth

I. Rule #1: Automate the Habit

"If it ain't automatic, it ain't consistent." – Big Tex

Set it. Forget it. Grow it.

◈ Use platforms like Vanguard, Schwab, Fidelity, SoFi, or Robinhood

◈ Link your checking account

◈ Set up auto-invest to buy:

- VTI (Total Market ETF)

- SCHD (Dividend Growth ETF)
- AAPL, MSFT, KO — your long-term horses

Minimum Monthly Target:

- $25 if you're broke
- $100 if you're steady
- $500 if you're serious

◈ Tex Talks:

"You'll never miss money that's already working."

II. Rule #2: The 10-Year Rule

Every time you buy an asset, ask:

> "Would I be fine holding this for 10 years... even if the market shut down tomorrow?"

If your answer is "No" — don't buy it.
If your answer is "Hell yes" — size your position and roll.

Think long, not loud. Quiet portfolios win wars.

III. Rule #3: Reinvest Dividends Like a Religion

Dividends are the compound fuel.

Example:

$10,000 in SCHD with a 3.5% dividend

→ Reinvested for 20 years

→ Grows to $21,143

→ Without dividends? Just $19,000

The real difference? The drip adds bricks to the wall.

◈ Tex Talks:

"Don't spend the golden goose's eggs — hatch them."

IV. Rule #4: Stop Checking the Damn Chart

You ain't a day trader. You're a wealth builder.
◈ Don't refresh your portfolio daily.
◈ Don't panic on red days.
◈ Check once a month to rebalance.
◈ Once a quarter to reassess strategy.
Emotion kills compounding.
If you're itching to click "sell" — step away from the screen.

V. Rule #5: Build the "No Matter What" Plan

Write this down:

"No matter what happens —

I will not sell out of fear

I will not stop my auto-investments

I will not listen to hype or doom

I will review my portfolio quarterly

I will trust the process"

Sign it. Date it. Tape it to your mirror, bunk, locker, or fridge.

This is your financial covenant.

VI. Rule #6: Buy the Drop, Bless the Dip

Every 12–18 months, the market dips 10–20%.

Here's what to do:

- Set aside "dry powder" (extra cash) monthly
- When the market tanks, buy more of what you already believe in
- Don't try to time the bottom — just buy the pain

◈ Tex Talks:

"Dips are discounts. Millionaires shop the red tags."

VII. Rule #7: Play the Long Game in Other Areas Too

The patient mindset bleeds into everything:

- Relationships: You don't rush love — you build it
- Health: You don't lose weight overnight — you earn it
- Reputation: You don't demand trust — you live it

Same with wealth.
Patience isn't passive. It's powerful.

VIII. Final Word: A Letter to the Impatient You

Dear Impatient You,

I know you want results fast.

I know you feel behind.

But if you rush this game, you'll lose the round and the board.

Wealth isn't built in moments. It's built in motions.

The question isn't how fast you can make it —

It's how long you're willing to become the kind of person who keeps it.

Stay in the game. Stack your patience. And never underestimate a man with a plan, a purpose, and a portfolio.

VII: The Power of Time — Inside the Math of Millionaires

Time is the quiet partner no one sees—until the check clears.

You don't need Wall Street genius. You don't need insider info. You need time and discipline. Here's what most people never learn:

I. Compound Interest: The Silent Juggernaut

> "Compound interest is the eighth wonder of the world." — Einstein

It's not a slogan. It's a formula:
FV = PV × (1 + r)^t

- FV = Future Value

- PV = Present Value (your investment)
- r = Interest Rate (average annual return)
- t = Time in years

Let's break it into real talk:

Starting Amount	Monthly Invested	Years	Return	Final Value
$0	$200	30	8%	$279,367
$5,000	$200	30	8%	$351,428
$0	$500	30	8%	$698,030
$0	$500	40	8%	$1,552,740

◈ Tex Talks:

"The money you think is crawling is actually sprinting — if you give it years instead of weekends."

II. The Time Penalty: What Waiting Costs You

Let's say you invest $300/month from age 25 to age 65. That's 40 years.

- 8% return = $933,974

Now let's say you wait until you're 35. Just 10 years late.

- 8% return = $407,145

Cost of procrastination?
$526,829
Ten years late = half a million lost.

◈ Tex Talks:

"Time doesn't take revenge. It just stops giving gifts."

III. The 15-Year Flip

You don't need 40 years to win.
Let's say you're 28, and you go hard:

- $500/month for 15 years
- 10% annual return
- No investing afterward

Then you let it sit until age 65.
That one 15-year run will grow to $1.5 million.
Compare that to investing $200/month for 40 years = $559,000.
It's not about how long you invest —
It's about how soon and how consistently you start.

IV. The Jailhouse Ledger

Let me take you back.
I sat with a man in Fremont Correctional Facility who was 42, 17 months from release. He said:

"I wasted my time. I've got nothing."

I handed him a pencil and a napkin.
We did the math.

- Start with $1,000
- Add $100/month
- Do that for 25 years
- 10% annual return = $139,889

Then we ran another one:

- Start at 42
- $300/month
- 25 years
- 10% return = $396,108

He stared at the number like it was an escape route.

⟐ Tex Talks:

"Your past ain't compound interest. Your future is. Start now."

V. Side-by-Side: Time vs. Hustle

Strategy	Start Age	Monthly	Years	Total Invested	Final Value (10%)
Early Bird	22	$300	10	$36,000	$637,000 at 65
Late Bloomer	35	$400	30	$144,000	$796,000 at 65
Aggressive Saver	40	$1,000	25	$300,000	$1.25 million

All of them win. But the early bird wins easiest.

VI. Don't Forget Taxes, Dividends & Reinvestment

This is clean math. But in real life:

- Dividends reinvested supercharge your returns
- Roth IRAs grow tax-free
- Index funds with low turnover = lower taxes

Example:
VTI (Total Market Index Fund) vs. GME (GameStop)

- VTI = 10% return, low taxes, low stress
- GME = 400% ride... but taxes hit, crash followed, emotion wrecked

One is a wealth plan. The other is a roller coaster.

◈ Tex Talks:

"Wall Street sells thrill rides. I sell train tracks. One gets you nowhere. One gets you home."

VII. Final Truth: Wealth Is Measured in Time, Not Toys

You don't need to be the richest man in the club.

You need to be the calmest man in the storm.

The man who doesn't flinch when layoffs come.

The woman who takes a sabbatical, not a second job.

The single mom who retires with dignity — not desperation.

That's what time buys you.

That's what patience creates.

That's what Chapter 9 delivers.

VIII: Final Reflections — What the Clock Is Really Ticking Toward

"Time is the friend of the wonderful business, the enemy of the mediocre." — Warren Buffett

But let me be straight with you: most people don't lose money in the markets because of the markets.

They lose because of the mirror.

They trade patience for dopamine.

They chase validation instead of value.
So let's talk truth.

I. Patience Isn't Passive — It's a Strategy

The market doesn't reward panic.
It doesn't care if your uncle says a crash is coming.
It doesn't move because you're nervous or bored.
The market rewards those who plant and wait.

> The farmer doesn't dig up the seeds when the rain comes.
>
> The builder doesn't quit when the concrete sets slow.
>
> The millionaire didn't make it from flipping — they made it from foundations.

II. The Quiet Power of Compound Character

This chapter ain't just about money.
It's about becoming the type of person who:

- Resists urgency
- Honors process
- Stays grounded when others get greedy
- Acts decisively, not emotionally

Because wealth is built by those who wait wisely, not those who wait weakly.

III. When Time Breaks You — Use It Anyway

Let me speak to the man in solitary.

Let me speak to the woman in Section 8 housing.

Let me speak to the kid hustling for lunch money.

You may not control your income right now.

You may not control your location.

But if you control your time — even a sliver of it — you control your outcome.

◈ Tex Talks:

"The game don't start when you get out. It starts the day you stop making excuses."

Even in prison, I made compound moves:

- I read 3 financial books a week
- I called in stock orders from commissary phones
- I used napkins and envelopes for budget journals

I built a war chest in the waiting room.

IV. Build with Time — Or Be Owned by It

You have a choice:

- You work for your time — clock in, clock out, spend life on someone else's schedule
- Or your time works for you — money moving 24/ 7, even while you sleep

The difference?

Patience.

Planning.

And starting when you feel the least ready.

V. Action Challenge: Commit to a 10-Year Wealth Habit

Do this now:

1. Write down one long-term financial goal (buy land, start a business, retire early)
2. Pick a single monthly investing amount (even $50)
3. Choose one simple long-term ETF (like VTI, SCHD, or QQQ)
4. Automate it
5. Don't touch it for a decade
6. Journal the journey every 90 days
7. Share this chapter with someone you trust

This is the blueprint. Not for overnight success — but for undeniable success.

VI. Final Word from Big Tex

"You're not late.

You're just on the wrong clock."

Change the timepiece.

Reset the rhythm.

Start walking in patience — and don't stop until your money moves without you.

Now turn the page.

CHAPTER 10: FINANCIAL STATEMENTS 101 – The Boardroom Battlefield

Section I: Why Financials Are Your Strategic Arsenal

⟐ Tex Talks:

"In the boardroom, numbers don't whisper—they declare war. If you don't speak their language, you'll always be the target, never the tactician."

1. The Myth of "Complex" Finance

Let's start with this: Wall Street wants you confused.

They want you intimidated by 10-Ks and terrified of accounting terms. Why? Because confusion is profitable—for them.

Here's the truth no one tells you:

- You don't need to be a CPA to read a balance sheet.
- You don't need calculus to understand cash flow.
- You need clarity, conviction, and the willingness to look past headlines.

Financial statements aren't math. They're strategy reports.

They reveal what a company really is—not what its marketing department wants you to believe.

Let me break it down simply:

Statement	What It Tells You	Why It Matters
Income Statement	Did they make or lose money?	Is the business viable, or just loud?
Balance Sheet	What do they own vs. what they owe?	Can they withstand volatility?
Cash Flow Statement	Are they managing liquidity well?	Is there real fuel behind the engine?

These three documents are the X-rays, MRIs, and blood tests of a business. Miss one, and you're guessing—not investing.

2. The Wharton Crucible: Learning to Skin a 10-K

I learned to dissect 10-Ks not in some fluorescent-lit basement or prison law library—I learned it at Wharton, at 3:07 a.m., in the Fischer Fine Arts Library, surrounded by men and women building billion-dollar blueprints.

My initiation came through a single company: Caterpillar Inc.

- Revenue was flat—no growth.
- Inventory was falling, but debt was climbing.
- That told me they were pushing backlog, not building momentum.

While the media praised their "resilience," I saw the warning signs.

◈ Tex Truth: "CEOs are storytellers. Financial statements are fact-checkers."

3. Why Wall Street Fears Educated Investors

Let's be blunt:

- Financial illiteracy feeds financial dependency.
- Most people scroll TikTok for stock tips but can't define gross margin.
- Retail investors chase hype. Institutions read footnotes.

> I built Carbonado Capital—now managing $700 million+—not on charisma, but on clarity.
>
> We trained our analysts to trust no one but the numbers. And it worked.

The moment you read your first 10-K cover to cover, you become dangerous. Because then, you see through the noise.

4. Financials: The Ultimate Bullsh*t Detector

Here's where fantasy meets reality:

Red Flag	Where to Find It	What It Means
"Record revenue" with declining margins	Income Statement	They're spending more to make less
High "adjusted EBITDA" with weak cash flow	Cash Flow Statement	Smoke and mirrors
Ballooning long-term debt	Balance Sheet	Leverage risk—especially in rising-rate environments

Case Study: WeWork (2019)

They claimed "growth," but bled billions. A quick scan of their cash flow told the real story: burn rates that would embarrass a startup.

> If you read what the markets ignore, you'll profit from what they panic over later.

5. The Ranch Parallel: From Herds to Holdings

Running Thomas Family Ranches taught me more about finance than any textbook. Because ranching is brutal economics. You learn fast or lose faster.

- Cattle inventory = Balance Sheet Assets

> Weak season? Cull low-yield producers. Just like underperforming divisions in a corporation.

- Corn futures = Risk Management

> Dry summer ahead? Lock in grain costs now. That's a hedge.

- Rain = Liquidity

> You don't plan for the drought in the drought—you plan during the flood.

⟐ Tex Lineage: "A rancher doesn't guess the weather. He reads the signs. Same with markets."

6. Legacy Builder: Yolanda's Financial Awakening

Meet Yolanda—a single mother from Dallas with a night shift nursing job and a dream to retire with dignity.

She attended one of my Financials for First-Timers workshops at Oak Cliff Community Hall.

Her breakthrough?

Reading McDonald's 10-K instead of watching talking heads.

> She found that 60% of McDonald's profit came not from burgers—but from real estate and franchise fees.

That changed her whole perspective.

- She started a dividend portfolio: KO, MCD, JNJ.
- Bought her first rental with the profits.
- Paid off her daughter's college education.

Today?

Yolanda has $281K in investments, three properties, and the knowledge to keep building.

◈ Tex Tribute: "She didn't need a fund manager. She needed the courage to open page one."

7. Action Challenge: Your Boardroom Initiation

Your mission isn't optional. If you want financial independence, you must learn to read power.

Do This Now:

1. Go to SEC.gov/EDGAR[1]
2. Search for Apple Inc.
3. Download their most recent 10-K Annual Report
4. Find these three key items:
    - Revenue (top line) → Are they growing?
    - Free Cash Flow → Are they efficient?
    - Debt-to-Equity Ratio → Are they overleveraged?
5. Write your interpretation in 150 words or less.
6. Email it to: BigTex@CarbonadoCapital.com

(Yes. I'll read it. Greatness demands accountability.)

◈ Tex Talks:

"They don't call me Big Tex for the boots. They call me that because I read what others skip. The edge isn't in guessing—it's in reading."

1. https://www.sec.gov/edgar

SECTION II: THE THREE CORE FINANCIAL STATEMENTS

What They Are. How They Lie. Why They Matter.

⟐ Tex Talks:

"Don't just read the numbers. Read what the numbers refuse to say. That's where the truth lives—and where your edge begins."

1. The Income Statement – The Illusion of Winning

Think of the income statement like a campaign rally: loud, impressive, and built to persuade.

- Revenue: The headliner. Everyone cheers when it's up.
- Net Income: The soundbite. "We made $1B this quarter!"
- Expenses: The buried fine print—where most companies hide their sins.

But smart investors? We read past the confetti:

- A company with rising revenue but declining gross margins? That's a business sprinting while bleeding internally.
- Big EPS (earnings per share) growth... but it's from stock buybacks, not real sales? That's a PR stunt,

not performance.

Tex Filter: Ask:

- Are they making money because of strong operations—or in spite of rising costs?
- Is revenue up but marketing spend skyrocketing? That's not growth. That's desperation.

◈ Tex Talks:

"In politics, they show you the polls. In business, they show you the income statement. In both cases—look for the margin of error."

2. The Balance Sheet – The Fortress or the Façade

This is the company's DNA. You want to know if a firm can take a punch? Look here.

- Assets: What they own.
- Liabilities: What they owe.
- Shareholder Equity: What's left if you subtract the two.

But raw numbers aren't enough. You need ratios:

- Current Ratio (Assets ÷ Liabilities): Can they pay short-term bills?
- Debt-to-Equity: Are they leveraged to grow... or to stay alive?
- Book Value per Share: What's your stake worth if

the whole thing shut down today?

Case Study – The WeWork Illusion:

In 2019, WeWork claimed massive valuation.

Their income statement looked shiny. But their balance sheet showed billions in lease liabilities.

- Assets were mostly hype-driven intangibles.
- Equity? Smoke and mirrors.
- Conclusion: the building looked good from the curb, but the foundation was sand.

◈ Tex Talks:

"When I look at a balance sheet, I don't see numbers I see survival odds."

3. The Cash Flow Statement – The Kingmaker

Forget profits. Cash is the lifeblood.

A company might say it's profitable, but if their cash flow is negative, they're on borrowed time.

Three Sections to Master:

- Operating Cash Flow: Money from core business. If this is negative run.
- Investing Cash Flow: Buying/selling assets. Expansion? Caution. Fire sale? Danger.
- Financing Cash Flow: Debt issued, dividends paid, stock bought back.

The Acid Test – Amazon vs. Enron:

- Amazon (2001): Net income negative, but strong operating cash flow. Long-term winner.
- Enron (2001): Net income positive, but cash flow screamed fraud.

Real cash never lies. Enron did.

◈ Tex Truth:

"The income statement is a suit and tie. The cash flow statement is the bank account password. One flatters. The other funds."

Quick Reference – The Executive Cheat Sheet

Statement	Focus	Red Flag to Watch
Income	Revenue & profits	Net income up, but margins shrinking
Balance Sheet	Assets vs. Liabilities	High debt-to-equity or collapsing equity
Cash Flow	Actual cash movement	Negative operating cash over multiple quarters

Why This Matters to You

Whether you're evaluating Apple stock or a local food truck, these statements give you control.

- Control over your money.
- Control over your decisions.
- Control over your future.

You're not just reading. You're interrogating. You're leading.

◈ Tex Talks:

"Every time I read a 10-K, I'm not asking what the company did—I'm asking what they're trying to hide."

III: How to Read a 10-K Like a Wall Street Insider

◈ Tex Talks:

"Most retail investors read headlines. Real investors read filings. You want alpha? It's buried on page 74 in footnote C."

1. The 10-K is the Investor's Battlefield Map

Let's get one thing clear:

- The 10-K isn't optional. It's your intel report.
- Wall Street analysts are trained to rip these apart—and they're betting you won't.

Here's what a 10-K really is:

Section	What It Tells You	Why It Matters
Business Overview	What they claim to do	Are they still relevant, or clinging to the past?
Risk Factors	What keeps them up at night	The real market dangers, in their own words
Management Discussion (MD&A)	The CEO's spin	How leadership justifies results—watch for linguistic gymnastics
Financial Statements	The data dump	Numbers don't lie. They whisper warnings.
Footnotes	The legal truth serum	Where the bodies are buried

Bottom line: If you're only reading the summary, you're investing blind.

2. My 10-Minute Triage Strategy

I've trained every analyst at Carbonado to master the 10-Minute Triage, a page-skimming protocol designed to sniff out opportunity—or catastrophe.

Here's how it goes:

1. Risk Factors (First Pass):
    - Highlight every phrase like "material weakness," "customer concentration," "supply chain disruption."
    - One red flag is a warning. Two? Dig deeper.
2. MD&A Language Patterns:

  - Watch for soft language: "may impact," "believe," "expected to improve." That's code for "we're guessing."
  - Direct language = confidence. Passive = panic.
3. Cash Flow Statement (Real Health Check):
  - Positive operating cash flow? Good.
  - Negative free cash flow + rising debt? Exit stage left.
4. Footnote Recon:
  - Go to the footnote on revenue recognition.
  - Any changes? Ask why.
  - Next, check pension obligations and lease liabilities. Off-balance-sheet debt hides here.

⟐ Tex Talks:

"If the CEO says 'everything is great' but the footnotes scream 'we're broke,' believe the footnotes."

3. Spotting the Red Flags Before They Cost You

Here's what we trained for in the war room:

Red Flag Phrase	What It Really Means	What To Do
"Going Concern"	They might go bankrupt	Do not invest
"Material Weakness in Controls"	Internal accounting may be broken	Proceed with extreme caution
"Customer Concentration"	One buyer = total exposure	Diversification risk
"Inventory Write-Down"	They overproduced, now eating losses	Check margins next
"Related Party Transactions"	Nepotism or self-dealing	Dig into governance

Investor Drill:

Open Amazon's latest 10-K. Search for "risk," "related," and "pension." What are they downplaying? What are they overemphasizing? Write it down. You're learning to think like Carbonado.

4. Legacy Builder: Malik's First 10-K

Malik, a 23-year-old barber from Houston, came to our Dallas seminar with zero investing experience. I handed him a 10-K for Nike. He said, "Man, I don't even know what I'm looking at."

We walked it together.

- He found R&D spending up 22% with flat revenue.
- "So they're betting on the future," he said.
- Two weeks later, he built a thesis: buy Nike on

weakness, long-term hold.

That was 2020. Today he's got:

- A $108K brokerage account
- A custom barber shop in South Dallas
- Four 10-Ks printed and marked up on his office wall

⟐ Tex Talks:

"He wasn't looking for tips. He was looking for truth. That's the investor mindset."

5. Action Challenge: The 10-K Gauntlet

Do This Now:

1. Pick any Fortune 500 company—preferably one you actually buy from.
2. Pull their 10-K from SEC.gov/EDGAR[2].
3. Identify and write down:
    - One risk factor that feels real
    - One financial number that looks strong
    - One footnote that raises an eyebrow
4. Start a 10-K journal. Track your insights. In 6 months, you'll read filings faster than most Ivy grads.

V: THE CASH FLOW STATEMENT – FOLLOW THE MONEY

⟐ Tex Talks:

2. https://www.sec.gov/edgar

"Profits lie. Cash don't. If you want to know what's really going on inside a company, follow the green."

If the income statement is a company's resume, the cash flow statement is its bank account login. It shows you what's real—not what's aspirational. You might hear that a company is "profitable," but if the cash isn't showing up in the bank, something's off. And as any rancher will tell you, a herd that looks good on paper don't mean much if you can't afford feed come winter.

The cash flow statement tracks how money moves through a business over a period of time. It answers a simple question: Did this company generate actual cash—or just shuffle numbers around?

There are three sections, and if you understand them, you'll see what the CEO wishes you didn't.

1. Operating Activities: The Business in Action

This is the engine. It's the core business—sales, expenses, taxes, the everyday grind. You want to see positive cash flow from operations. If a company can't make money from what it actually does, it's in trouble.

When I analyze a business, this section gets my first 10 minutes. If operating cash is negative for multiple quarters while revenue is rising, I dig deeper. Are they overextending? Masking deeper inefficiencies?

I once passed on a buzzy AI startup that posted positive net income but had negative operating cash flow for three straight quarters. The reason? Deferred revenue games and stock-based compensation tricks. I walked away. Two quarters later, they missed earnings and got clobbered 32%. Cash told the truth before the earnings call ever did.

◈ Tex Talks:

"I'd rather back a boring company with cash in the tank than a 'hot' one running on fumes. Momentum doesn't pay the bills—liquidity does."

2. Investing Activities: Skin in the Game or a Fire Sale?

This section tells you how a company is investing its money—buying assets, expanding operations, acquiring competitors. If you see large outflows here, it's not automatically bad. It could mean growth, vision, ambition.

But context matters.

Let's say a company is hemorrhaging cash in investing activities but has flat or negative operating cash flow. That's not bold—it's reckless.

I once reviewed a regional telecom that spent $800 million upgrading its fiber network in a two-year window. Sounds impressive—until I noticed they hadn't posted positive operating cash flow since the upgrades began. They were lighting matches with investor money. I shorted them. Three months later, they slashed guidance and laid off 12% of staff. Again: cash was the canary.

Now, there are times I'll greenlight a short-term cash flow sacrifice for long-term upside. I did it with Deere & Co. during their acquisition of a precision ag startup. Why? Because their operating cash stayed strong. They could afford the move.

3. Financing Activities: Who's Writing the Checks?

Here's where the real poker game begins.

This section shows how a company funds its operations—debt, equity raises, dividends, stock buybacks. It tells you who's backing the play... and who's getting paid.

If you see massive inflows from financing, ask yourself: Are they borrowing because they're growing—or because they're bleeding?

One of my biggest red flags? Companies raising equity—selling new shares—while their stock is soaring. That's called dilution. You might be making gains, but your ownership percentage is shrinking. Quiet theft, dressed as growth.

A perfect example? AMC Entertainment during the meme stock craze. The company raised billions issuing new stock when its price was artificially inflated by Reddit hype. Smart move for them. A sucker punch for shareholders who bought the lie.

◈ Tex Talks:

"If a company's issuing stock while screaming 'we're undervalued!'—believe their actions, not their tweets."

Putting It All Together: The Real Story Isn't in One Line

A rookie investor looks at net income. A professional looks at the cash flow from operations.

But the Carbonado way? We read all three sections in tension. We look for contradictions. Disguises. Gaps between words and wallets.

I've seen companies show positive net income but borrow heavily to fund dividend payouts. That's not generosity. That's optics.

Others show massive negative cash from investing—but their operating cash is soaring. That's not a crisis. That's expansion.

The point is, this statement doesn't care about brand reputation, product buzz, or executive charisma. It cares about one thing: Where did the money actually go?

And if you learn to follow it—really follow it—you'll never look at a balance sheet, a press release, or a stock chart the same way again.

⟐ Tex Talks:

"I wasn't raised broke—I was raised sharp. I didn't follow cash because I had to. I followed it because that's how leaders think. Cash isn't backup—it's the blueprint."

VI: The Footnotes – Where the Bodies Are Buried

Financial statements may tell a story, but the footnotes reveal the truth. That's where companies disclose the fine print—what they hope you'll skip, skim, or outright ignore. But if you're serious about investing like a professional, this is where you learn to read like a prosecutor, not a fanboy.

Every company that files with the SEC includes notes to their financial statements—dozens of pages that explain how they calculated key figures, what accounting assumptions they used, and where potential landmines are buried. If the income statement is the press release, the footnotes are the sworn testimony.

◈ Tex Talks:

"If the CEO is the salesman, the footnotes are the receipts. Read them. That's where the lies get softened, the losses get buried, and the risk gets real."

Reading the Red Flags

Here's what I look for, and what I train my analysts to hunt without mercy:

1. Accounting Method Changes

When a company suddenly shifts from one accounting method to another—say, from FIFO to LIFO inventory accounting—it's often not innovation. It's camouflage. They're usually trying to smooth over a bad quarter, inflate margins, or defer taxes. And guess what? Most retail investors never notice.

2. Contingent Liabilities

This is where lawsuits live. Product recalls. Government investigations. Environmental cleanup risks. A company might be facing a billion-dollar lawsuit and bury it in Note 14 with the phrase: "We believe the resolution of this matter will not have a material impact on our operations." Read that again. Believe. Not have. Material. Legalese for: "We don't know, and we hope you won't either."

3. Revenue Recognition Games

Look closely when a company starts counting revenue sooner than it should. You'll often see phrases like "estimated completion method" or "percentage of completion." Translation: They're booking future sales as if they already happened. That's not revenue. That's wishful thinking.

4. Off-Balance-Sheet Financing

Some companies keep debts hidden through creative entities, joint ventures, or leasing structures. It's technically legal. Ethically? That's another story. Think Enron. Think Lehman Brothers. Think caution.

My First Footnote Wake-Up Call

Back at Wharton, we were dissecting the 10-K of a multinational construction firm. Everyone was praising their free cash flow and robust EBITDA. I flipped to Note 17 and saw it: a pending lawsuit in Brazil over labor violations and environmental damages that, if resolved against them, would wipe out three quarters of profits. No one else caught it.

That moment taught me more than any finance professor. From then on, I never read a 10-K without hitting the footnotes first.

◈ Tex Talks:

"Want to spot the iceberg before the Titanic sinks? Stop staring at the champagne and read the structural report. That's what the footnotes are."

Carbonado's Internal Rule

At Carbonado Capital, we have a non-negotiable: No investment is approved unless the footnotes have been read in full and cross-referenced with public disclosures. Period.

Every analyst on our team learns this discipline. I don't care how bullish the chart looks or how glowing the earnings call was—if the footnotes contradict the narrative, we walk.

Because if you want to play at this level, you don't get excited by headlines. You get surgical with filings.

Case in Point: The Dropbox Decision

A few years back, Dropbox was flying high. Cloud storage was hot. Revenue was growing. Tech influencers were salivating. But in the footnotes, I spotted an obscure line about capitalized software development costs—rising fast, year over year. It meant they were burying costs in intangible assets, artificially boosting profits.

We passed. Six months later, earnings missed, the stock fell 18%, and every talking head on CNBC was "surprised."

We weren't.

◈ Tex Talks:

"Never invest in a company whose footnotes you haven't read. That's not due diligence. That's gambling in a suit."

VII: Legacy Builder – Yolanda's Financial Awakening

◈ Tex Talks:

"Most people wait for a miracle. Yolanda read the damn report."

Yolanda Matthews didn't look like your average investor—and that was the point. Forty-three years old, night-shift nurse, single mom to a teenage daughter with a love for books and a dream of college. She wasn't flashy, wasn't loud, and she'd never owned a share of stock in her life.

She walked into my Financials for First-Timers seminar on a Saturday morning wearing scrubs and carrying a $2 notebook. She sat in the back, took notes like her life depended on it, and never once touched her phone. I noticed.

At the end of the seminar, she didn't ask about stock tips or hot sectors. She asked about franchise margins in McDonald's 10-K. That's when I knew she was different.

> "If 60% of McDonald's profits come from franchising, why does the media only talk about burgers?" she asked.
>
> I smiled. "Because flash sells. But cash stays."
>
> She nodded. "So... the game isn't food. It's real estate and fees."
>
> "Exactly. You just decoded the business model with a single paragraph."

That night, she went home and read the full 124-page filing. The next week, she emailed me her analysis—broken down, cross-referenced, and bulletproof. She wasn't guessing. She was auditing capitalism.

From Nurse to Navigator

Yolanda didn't have a brokerage account, so we helped her open one through a platform that allowed fractional shares. Her first investment? $117 into McDonald's (MCD), spread over two weeks. She reinvested her dividends. Then she bought Johnson & Johnson— "not because of Band-Aids," she told me, "But because their R&D pipeline is loaded with FDA-phase products. That's cash flow waiting to happen."

Within nine months, she had $2,200 in her account. By year two: $18,400. And by the time her daughter got her acceptance letter to Vanderbilt University, Yolanda had:

- Built a six-month emergency fund
- Acquired three cash-flowing rental properties
- Accumulated over $281,000 in a diversified investment portfolio

She never once chased hype. She read. She understood. She moved.

What Set Her Apart

She treated her portfolio like her patients—with care, data, and no shortcuts. She didn't follow the noise. She followed the numbers. She told me, "I realized if I could understand a patient's chart, I could understand a company's. One is anatomy. The other is accounting."

She was right.

⟐ Tex Talks:

"Legacy doesn't require a windfall. It requires a willingness to read what others ignore. Yolanda's daughter didn't get lucky—she got led."

Why Yolanda Matters

She wasn't a finance pro. She was a working mom who got tired of living at the mercy of late shifts and rising rent. Her power didn't come from Wall Street connections or a fat inheritance—it came from learning to decipher the truth inside a 10-K.

Yolanda is proof that this book isn't theory. It's blueprint.

If you can read, you can own. If you can interpret, you can invest. If you can act, you can change your legacy.

She did.

And now?

She teaches her daughter to do the same.

VIII: Action Challenge – Your Boardroom Initiation

◈ Tex Talks:

"Most people scroll headlines. Investors read filings. If you're still chasing opinions, you're not building ownership—you're building excuses."

This is where the rubber meets the ranch road.

You've studied the battlefield:

- The Income Statement (Your profit pulse)
- The Balance Sheet (Your financial foundation)
- The Cash Flow Statement (Your economic engine)
- And the Footnotes (Your BS detector)

Now, it's time to act. This section isn't about passive reading. It's your first step into real financial literacy—the kind that doesn't just change your understanding, it changes your outcomes.

Here's your personal challenge from me to you—no fluff, no gimmicks, no social media hype. Just the work.

Your Mission: Become a Boardroom Insider

You are now the CEO of your portfolio. That means understanding a company like a boss, not a bystander.

Do this today. Not tomorrow. Not after brunch. Now.

Step 1: Visit SEC.gov/EDGAR

This is where all public companies file their annual reports (10-Ks). No paywall. No clickbait. Just raw data—your new best friend.

Step 2: Download Apple's Latest 10-K

Why Apple? Because it's the most valuable company on Earth—and one of the most misunderstood. You've bought their products. Now read their blueprint.

Step 3: Find and Interpret Three Critical Elements

1. Revenue Trends
    - Look at the top line over the past 3 years.
    - Are they still growing? Is it organic or acquisition-driven?
    - What division is driving the gains—hardware, services, international markets?
2. Free Cash Flow
    - Find the Cash Flow Statement and subtract capital expenditures from operating cash.
    - Are they generating consistent free cash flow?
    - Is it rising, stable, or volatile?
3. Debt-to-Equity Ratio
    - Locate total liabilities and total shareholder equity on the Balance Sheet.
    - Divide debt by equity.
    - Is Apple taking on smart leverage or

bloating its books?

Step 4: Reflect and Write

In a notebook—or better yet, your investing journal—answer these questions:

- What surprised you most?
- What risk do you see that headlines missed?
- Would you invest in Apple right now based on the financials alone?

◈ Tex Talks:

"I've read more 10-Ks in prison libraries than most hedge fund managers do in their offices. Why? Because ownership doesn't wait on freedom. It starts with discipline."

Bonus Challenge: Send It to Me

If you're bold, send your breakdown to: BigTex@CarbonadoCapital.com

I don't promise a response. But I promise you this—every email gets read.

Legacy Builder's Pledge

Write this on the first page of your financial notebook:

> "I will not invest in what I don't understand. I will read the filings. I will learn the language of ownership. Because my family's future deserves more than guesses."

Sign it. Date it. Frame it if you have to.

This is your line in the sand. You've now crossed it.

CHAPTER 11: THE HIDDEN LANGUAGE OF VALUATION – What the Market Really Pays For

I: Price Ain't Value – And Why Most People Confuse the Two

◈ Tex Talks:

"A $2 stock can be overpriced. A $300 stock can be a steal. That's the difference between trading and thinking."

If you don't learn anything else from this chapter, learn this:

Price is just a number. Value is the truth hiding beneath it.

Most people walk into the stock market like they're strolling through a clearance rack.

— "Ooh, this one's under $10, must be cheap."

— "That one's $450? No way I can afford that."

They're not investing. They're bargain hunting with blinders on.

Let me break it to you straight:

The stock market isn't Walmart. It's a damn auction house.

And in an auction, the highest bid doesn't always match the worth of the item—it matches the emotion of the buyer.

I. Price is What You Pay. Value is What You Own.

That's not just a catchy phrase—it's the cornerstone of wealth-building.

Price is what the market—meaning other people—are willing to pay at this moment.

Value is what the business is actually worth, based on its future cash flows, assets, competitive position, and risk profile.

Markets move on emotion. Value stands on fundamentals.

Imagine buying a ranch. The seller asks $2 million.

Before you sign, you're going to ask:

- How much land am I getting?
- What's the water situation?
- How many head of cattle can it support?
- Are there oil or mineral rights?

If the answer to all those is strong—you might even pay above asking.

If it's all smoke and dry soil—you walk, no matter the price.

That's valuation. Not what's written on the tag, but what's under the hood.

II. The Fallacy of "Cheap Stocks"

Let me introduce you to the penny stock graveyard. It's littered with so-called "cheap" stocks that went to zero:

- Blockbuster Video: "Too cheap to fail." It failed.
- RadioShack: "Legacy brand." Legacy losses.
- Sears: "It's a household name!" And now it's gone.

They weren't "cheap"—they were dying.

The price reflected the market's gut feeling, but it didn't tell the full story. That's where you come in.

Owning shares isn't about affordability—it's about understanding what you're buying.

A $10 stock with no earnings and declining revenue? That's overpriced.

A $400 stock with consistent cash flow, low debt, and market dominance? That might be a discount.

◈ Tex Talks:

"If price is the sticker on the windshield, value is the engine under the hood. You buying paint or horsepower?"

III. Amazon vs. Pets.com – A Lesson Burned into My DNA

Let's rewind to 2001. The dot-com bubble had just burst. Everyone was dumping tech like it was radioactive.

Pets.com was everywhere—ads, TV spots, even the Super Bowl. It was "cheap" on paper.

Amazon? It was bleeding red ink and trading at levels people called "insane."

But I wasn't looking at the stock chart. I was reading the filings. Amazon had:

- Infrastructure.
- Logistics.
- Repeat customers.
- Vision.

Pets.com had...a sock puppet.

By 2002, Pets.com was bankrupt. Amazon? Still standing. Now a trillion-dollar empire.

> "That lesson wasn't learned in a cell—it was crystallized at Wharton, confirmed on the ranch, and proven in every boardroom where I've run the numbers. I've seen overpriced hype implode and undervalued giants roar back. That's the edge—knowing the difference before the crowd does."

IV. Why the Herd Gets It Wrong

Let me pull the curtain back:

- The media pushes price stories, not value stories.
- Influencers post "$100 to $10,000" overnight wins, not balance sheet breakdowns.
- Most retail investors? They're buying emotion, not equity.

The market punishes emotion and rewards discipline.

You're not here to gamble. You're here to own.

And ownership starts with understanding what you're paying for—and why it's worth it.

V. The Rancher's Eye: How I Size Up Value

When I buy cattle, I don't just look at the hide. I check the legs, the lungs, the breeding history.

When I buy a company, I do the same thing. I don't care about the chart. I care about:

- The moat (How hard is it to compete with?)
- The management (Do they allocate capital like ranchers or riverboat gamblers?)
- The margins (Are they surviving or thriving?)
- The debt (Are they riding high or just highly leveraged?)

A good company on sale is a rare thing. But when it happens—you don't hesitate. You load the truck.

◈ Tex Talks:

"They say buy low, sell high. I say buy value, hold tight, and let the world catch up to your vision."

II: P/E, P/B, and the Alphabet Soup of Metrics

◈ Tex Talks:

"Valuation metrics aren't magic—they're just math. But in the right hands, they're a scalpel, not a shovel. Use them to dissect a business, not bury your capital."

Every seasoned investor eventually learns: the market speaks in numbers—and those numbers tell stories.

But too many investors quote metrics without context. They say "low P/E is good" or "high P/B is bad" like parrots at a trading convention. Real valuation requires discernment. The numbers don't exist in a vacuum. They exist in a living, breathing business with moving parts and market cycles.

Here's how to read those metrics like a pro—not a poseur.

1. P/E Ratio (Price-to-Earnings)

Formula:

Price per Share ÷ Earnings per Share

This tells you how many dollars investors are willing to pay for each dollar of current earnings. A P/E of 15 means you're paying $15 for every $1 the company earns in profit.

But here's the problem:

A "low" P/E can mean two things:

- ◈ A value opportunity
- ◈ A business in decline

And a "high" P/E?

- ◈ A company with high growth expectations
- ◈ A bubble waiting to pop

Tex Example:

Back in 2014, I passed on a small-cap tech stock trading at a P/E of 9. Sounded cheap—until I read the earnings call transcript. Revenue was shrinking, customer churn was high, and they were cutting R&D. That wasn't value. That was decay.

2. P/B Ratio (Price-to-Book)

Formula:

Price per Share ÷ Book Value per Share

This one shows how the market values a company compared to its net assets. A ratio below 1 could mean the company is trading below the value of its assets. But again—context matters.

- In capital-heavy industries (like banking or insurance), a low P/B can flag hidden value.
- In IP-driven industries (like software or biotech), P/B might be nearly irrelevant. Their real value isn't on the balance sheet—it's in code, patents, and people.

Tex Truth:

I never rely on P/B alone—but when I'm scanning for undervalued financials or old-school industrials, it's one of my first filters. If the balance sheet is strong and the price is lagging, I start digging.

3. PEG Ratio (Price/Earnings to Growth)

Formula:

P/E Ratio ÷ Annual EPS Growth

This adjusts the P/E by factoring in the company's growth rate. A PEG of 1.0 is considered "fair value." Below 1.0? Possibly undervalued. Above 1.0? Possibly overpriced—or priced for perfection.

But here's what most people miss: growth quality matters more than growth speed.

Is it margin-accretive? Sustainable? Backed by cash flow?

Tex Checkpoint:

I once turned down a hot med-tech stock with a "PEG of 0.6." Everyone called it a steal. But their growth was fueled by acquisitions, not organic performance. When interest rates jumped, the whole thing collapsed. PEG meant nothing without real analysis.

4. EV/EBITDA (Enterprise Value to Earnings Before Interest, Taxes, Depreciation, and Amortization)

This is how professionals value companies with complex capital structures or high debt.

- Enterprise Value = Market Cap + Debt – Cash
- EBITDA = A proxy for operating cash flow

A lower EV/EBITDA ratio can suggest a bargain—but you'd better ask why it's low. This is where distressed assets hide.

Use this when:

- Comparing companies with different levels of debt
- Evaluating potential acquisitions
- Judging operational profitability without accounting noise

◈ Tex Talks:

"Metrics don't lie—but liars use metrics. Know the business, then confirm it with the ratios—not the other way around."

The Real Power in the Ratios

Valuation ratios aren't prescriptions. They're tools.

They don't tell you what to buy. They tell you where to look.

And when used properly—with full knowledge of the business, the sector, and the cycle—they can give you the confidence to invest with conviction while the crowd is still chasing headlines.

III: What Smart Money Actually Looks At

◈ Tex Talks:

"Retail chases noise. Institutions read the fine print. If you want institutional returns, you've got to train your eyes like an insider."

There's a reason the average retail investor underperforms the market—and it's not lack of opportunity.

It's lack of focus.

While the herd stares at the price chart, the smart money—the hedge funds, private equity firms, seasoned portfolio managers—are asking different questions:

- Where's the free cash flow headed?
- Is this business mispriced due to temporary noise?
- Who's buying the stock... and who's quietly exiting?

This section pulls back the curtain on how real capital allocators think—and what you should start paying attention to if you want to play at that level.

1. Free Cash Flow – The Gold Standard

Forget reported earnings.

Smart investors chase Free Cash Flow (FCF)—the cash a company generates after expenses and reinvestment.

Why?

Because earnings can be massaged. FCF is harder to fake.

> Free Cash Flow = Operating Cash Flow – Capital Expenditures

This is what determines whether a company can:

- Pay dividends
- Repurchase shares
- Pay down debt
- Acquire competitors
- Survive a downturn

Tex Insight:

I once greenlit a $5M investment in a manufacturing firm despite weak GAAP earnings. Why? Because their free cash flow was rock solid hidden beneath temporary accounting write-downs. Two years later, they got acquired for a 62% premium.

2. Insider Buying – The Quiet Signal

When a CEO sells shares, it could mean anything—estate planning, diversification, taxes.

But when a CEO buys shares on the open market?

That means one thing: conviction.

Smart money tracks insider activity like a hawk. If multiple senior execs are loading up? That's often a sign the market is undervaluing something long-term.

Look for:

- Cluster buying (several insiders at once)
- Size (Is it meaningful relative to their net worth?)
- Timing (Is it during a selloff?)

Red flag? Insiders selling right before bad news. That's a clue to walk—not run—from the stock.

3. Institutional Accumulation – The Whale Watch

Big funds don't move quickly. They scale into positions over weeks, sometimes months, to avoid moving the market.

That's why smart money watches:

- 13F filings (quarterly disclosures of institutional holdings)
- Unusual options volume (often a hint of big-money hedging or positioning)
- Volume spikes with little news (someone's buying quietly)

If a $20B fund is slowly building a stake in a boring utility company, they're not doing it for thrills. They've run the models, stress-tested the margins, and seen something the crowd missed.

Tex Rule:

When a whale circles, don't jump in the water unless you know what they're hunting.

4. Capital Allocation Strategy

Here's the real test of management quality: What do they do with your money once they've earned it?

Smart money evaluates companies like investment funds:

- Are they buying back shares at attractive valuations?
- Are they reinvesting in high-return projects?
- Are they raising the dividend consistently—but responsibly?
- Are they overpaying for acquisitions just to buy growth?

This is the difference between a business owner's mindset and a stock flipper's mindset. You want to be in business with leaders who know how to compound capital, not just chase headlines.

◈ Tex Talks:

"I don't just invest in companies—I invest in decision-makers. And I don't care if their title says CEO or CFO. If they can't allocate capital, they don't get mine."

5. Moats, Not Hype

Warren Buffett didn't become the GOAT by chasing trends—he hunted moats:

- Pricing power
- Brand loyalty
- Network effects
- Switching costs
- Scale efficiencies

Smart money looks beyond today's buzzwords and asks:

> "How hard would it be for a new player to beat this company at its own game?"

If the answer is "damn near impossible," you might be looking at a long-term compounder.

In Summary:

Smart money doesn't need to check stock tickers every 5 minutes.

Why? Because they've done the work. They understand value, not just price.

They own businesses, not just shares.

Want to play at that level?

Learn to think like them.

Build conviction.

And stop chasing candles on a chart.

IV: Valuing a Business from the Ground Up – The Carbonado Way

◈ Tex Talks:

"At Carbonado, we didn't value companies the way Wall Street taught—we valued them the way owners do: with skin in the game, time on the line, and zero tolerance for fantasy."

You've read about valuation ratios, cash flow metrics, and institutional signals. But theory without method is just noise.

Let me show you how we do it at Carbonado Capital.

This is the Carbonado Protocol—our internal framework for valuing companies with discipline and clarity. It's not about formulas—it's about frameworks that make money.

1. Start with the Business, Not the Stock

Before we even look at the ticker symbol, we ask:

- What do they actually sell?
- Who is their real customer?
- What pain are they solving—and is that pain getting worse or going away?
- How hard would it be for me—or someone smarter than me—to replicate this business?

We treat every public company like a private investment. Because if you wouldn't own the whole business outright, you shouldn't own even one share.

2. Score the Company Across Five Core Pillars

We developed a proprietary rubric that scores every company on a scale of 1–10 in five categories:

Pillar	What We Measure	Example
Market Risk	Sensitivity to macro trends, competition	A homebuilder in a rising rate environment gets a 7; a discount grocer in a recession gets a 3
Company Risk	Management integrity, operational strength	Founder-led with skin in the game? That's a 2. Bloated board and activist pressure? That's an 8
Financial Health	Debt load, cash flow consistency, margin trend	We score weak EBITDA margins or lumpy cash flow higher for risk
Valuation Risk	Is the stock overpriced relative to actual value?	A software company at 80x sales gets flagged, even with growth
Emotional Bias	Are we being seduced by brand, media, or narrative?	We call this the "Tesla Test." If you're too excited, step back

A total risk score above 25? No-go. Below 20? It's in the bullpen for deeper due diligence.

3. Run Scenarios, Not Predictions

We don't "predict the future"—we pressure test possible futures.

Scenario Planning:

- What happens if rates jump 200 basis points?
- What if China bans their product overnight?
- What if a key exec resigns?
- What if a once-in-a-decade storm halts production?

If the business still stands strong under pressure, we consider it durable.

If the thesis crumbles with one bad headline? That's not investment-grade—it's narrative hype.

4. Establish the Edge—or Pass

We don't invest unless we see a clear, sustainable edge—information, timing, or insight the market hasn't priced in yet.

- Are we early to a trend Wall Street's ignoring?
- Have we uncovered something buried in an obscure footnote?
- Do we have network intel—supplier feedback, leadership history, real-world friction?

If we can't answer why this stock, why now, then we don't move.

◈ Tex Talks:

"No edge? No entry. Don't bet your capital on hope—bet it on something the market missed."

5. Decide Entry, Exit, and Guardrails Before Clicking Buy

Before we even touch the "buy" button, we define:

- ◈ Entry Price Range (based on intrinsic value, not chart patterns)
- ◈ Exit Strategy (long-term hold, takeover target, price trigger)
- ◈ Risk Guardrails (stop-loss, position size, time horizon)

This is where most investors fail. They buy first, plan later.

We plan first. Then we strike.

Tex Rule:

"Your worst investment decisions come when you feel smartest. Bake in humility before you buy."

6. Example: The Lennar Trade

Lennar Corporation (LEN), a top U.S. homebuilder, hit our radar in a rising-rate environment when housing sentiment was shaky.

- Market Risk: 5 (rates up, but inventory down)
- Company Risk: 2 (strong leadership, clear backlog)
- Financial Health: 3 (robust free cash flow, disciplined leverage)
- Valuation Risk: 4 (trading under book value on rate fears)
- Emotional Bias: 1 (no media hype, just fundamentals)

Total Risk Score: 15

Result: We initiated a position at $64. Three quarters later, the stock hit $112.

Not because we timed the market. Because we understood the business better than the market did.

Final Word on Valuation

Valuation isn't a spreadsheet exercise. It's a discipline.

It's what separates gamblers from builders, speculators from strategists.

You don't need 10 screens. You need clarity, conviction, and a framework that keeps you honest.

That's what the Carbonado Protocol gave us. And now, you've got it too.

V: When the Market Misprices Greatness – Contrarian Conviction

◈ Tex Talks:

"The crowd has a short memory and a weak stomach. If you've got the patience to stand alone, you'll often be the only one left at the finish line—with everything."

If there's one enduring truth about markets, it's this:

> Price is not the same as value.

Stocks get mispriced all the time—sometimes because of panic, sometimes because of hype, and often because the market just doesn't know how to interpret the data yet.

That's where contrarian conviction comes in.

You don't build wealth by following the herd. You build it by standing apart from it—armed with discipline, data, and a time horizon longer than next Friday.

1. What Does It Mean to Be Contrarian?

Being contrarian doesn't mean being a reflexive pessimist. It means thinking independently.

- When a great company is getting hammered for temporary issues, contrarians buy.
- When everyone's euphoric over a stock they don't understand, contrarians take profits—or walk away.
- When the market ignores a business because it's "boring," contrarians dig deeper.

Contrarian conviction is not about disagreeing for the sake of it.

It's about being early, being right, and being willing to look wrong for a while.

2. What the Crowd Gets Wrong

Markets are emotional machines. They overreact.

- Bad quarter? Panic sell.
- CEO scandal? Dump it all.
- Negative headlines? Assume apocalypse.

But great investors don't chase headlines—they read the footnotes.

They know the difference between permanent damage and temporary noise.

Case Study: Target Corporation (TGT) in 2020

During the George Floyd protests, Target was hit hard—stores closed, looting occurred, the stock dropped.

But we ran the numbers:

- Inventory turnover was accelerating.
- E-commerce growth was exploding.
- Their supply chain was already retooled post-COVID.

While others sold in fear, we saw a logistics powerhouse getting discounted for a short-term event.

We bought at $117.

18 months later? It was trading north of $250.

That wasn't luck. That was conviction backed by data.

3. Contrarianism Requires Preparation

You can't just go "against the grain" without a thesis. You'll get crushed.

True contrarian investing requires:

- Deep knowledge of the business model
- Familiarity with the balance sheet
- Understanding of industry cycles
- A clear exit strategy before you buy

In other words, it's not rebellion—it's research.

4. The Emotional Toll of Being Early

Let's not sugarcoat it—being a contrarian is hard. You'll look foolish before you look brilliant.

- Your friends will doubt you.
- CNBC will scream that you're wrong.
- The stock may fall further before it climbs.

But if you've done the work, your conviction will hold. And when the market catches up? You'll already be positioned.

Tex Principle:

"Every wealth-building decision I ever made looked crazy at the start. That's how I knew it had potential."

5. How to Build Contrarian Conviction

Here's how we trained our team at Carbonado to develop this edge:

- Read the 10-K first, the news second.
- Identify the narrative mismatch. What is the market missing?
- Stress test the thesis. What happens if you're early? What's the real downside?
- Track sentiment, not just fundamentals. When everyone's on one side of the boat, the boat tips.

6. Legacy Builder Spotlight: Mark – The Railroad Man

Mark was a blue-collar union worker who started following my newsletter in 2017. He didn't care for crypto or startups—but he understood trains.

In 2020, CSX Corporation dipped 30% on earnings fears and fuel price volatility. The crowd fled.

But Mark read the filing:

- Operating ratio improving
- Intermodal contracts expanding
- Dividend secure

He doubled down at $58. Three years later? $100+.

He didn't have a finance degree. He had conviction grounded in understanding.

◈ Tex Talks:

"You don't need a Bloomberg terminal. You need clarity, courage, and a company you understand better than anyone."

Why This Matters

Most investors spend their lives chasing approval—confirmation from the market, the media, the mob.

But wealth doesn't follow the crowd.

It waits quietly at the far end of reason—where only the prepared contrarian is willing to go.

You don't have to be loud.

You just have to be right—when it counts.

VI: Action Plan – Valuation in the Wild

⟐ Tex Talks:

"This is where the talk stops and the trade begins. You've got the knowledge. Now it's time to prove you can wield it."

It's one thing to understand valuation from a textbook. It's another to walk into the real world—armed only with your judgment, your framework, and your ability to tune out the noise—and make an investment call when no one else will.

Here's how we translate the theory into execution.

1. Build Your Valuation Toolkit

Before you attempt to value a stock, gather your tools:

- Latest 10-K filing (from SEC.gov/EDGAR)
- Most recent quarterly earnings call transcript
- Balance sheet, income statement, cash flow summary
- Three-year trend of revenue, margins, and debt
- Ownership breakdown (insiders, institutions, float)

You don't need fancy software. You need focus and a framework.

Your job? Find where the story and the numbers don't match.

2. Choose a Company—Not a Stock

Stop thinking in tickers. Think in businesses. Choose a company you either already use, admire, or understand deeply.

- Eat Chick-fil-A every week? Study Yum! Brands (they own competitors).
- Obsessed with gaming? Look at NVIDIA or Activision.
- Former trucker? Dig into J.B. Hunt or Old Dominion.

The edge is personal insight. Don't outsource your curiosity.

3. Run the Carbonado Protocol (Condensed)

Take the business you chose and apply the risk scoring method:

Pillar	Notes	Score
Market Risk.	What's the industry cycle? Recession-proof?	
Company Risk	Management? Lawsuits? Turnover?	
Financial Health	Debt vs. cash? Margin compression?	
Valuation Risk	P/E high? Priced for perfection?	
Emotional Bias	Are you falling in love with the brand?	

Total Score: _______

Guideline: If it's over 25, walk. If it's under 20, you've got a research candidate.

4. Write a One-Page Thesis

No more than one page. No fluff. Just clarity.

- What's the business?
- Why is it undervalued?
- What are the key risks—and how are they being mitigated?
- What's the upside potential?
- What's your exit plan?

If you can't explain it simply, you don't understand it yet.
◈ Tex Talks:
"If it can't fit on one page, it's not a thesis—it's a fantasy."

5. Take the "Paper Trade" Challenge

Before putting real money down, test your conviction.

- Log the company, entry price, your risk score, and your one-page thesis.
- Set your target price and exit plan.
- Track it over the next 90 days.
- Journal your emotional reactions—especially when the stock moves against you.

This isn't about winning. It's about watching how you handle pressure, second-guessing, and doubt.

6. The Legacy Builder Pledge

Take this seriously. Write it down and sign it.

> "I pledge never to buy a company I haven't studied. I will not trade on hype. I will not chase charts. I will value businesses, think long-term, and protect my capital like it's my family's legacy—because it is."

Sign it. Tape it above your desk.

Let it check your emotions before every trade.

7. Final Assignment: Show Me What You've Got

Pick one company you believe is undervalued today.

Apply the full process.

Send me your write-up at: BigTex@CarbonadoCapital.com

Yes, I'll read it.

Yes, some of you will get personal feedback.

Yes, this could change the trajectory of your financial future.

◈ Tex Talks:

"Valuation isn't theory—it's how we build dynasties. You either learn the game or get played by it. I chose the first path. Now you can too."

Chapter 12: Dividends – Getting Paid to Be Patient

I: The Power of Boring Money

◈ Tex Talks:

"They mocked me for loving dividends. Said it was 'slow money.' I smiled, cashed the checks, and watched my portfolio outpace theirs—with less drama."

Ask most new investors what excites them about the stock market, and you'll hear talk about explosive growth, ten-baggers, or the next Tesla. But ask the wealthiest, most consistent investors what built their empires? You'll hear one quiet word:

Dividends.

Dividends are the financial backbone of the patient investor. They don't come with fanfare, social media buzz, or speculative thrill. But they compound. They accumulate. They quietly snowball into wealth—especially when reinvested.

Here's what most people miss:

> Dividends aren't just income—they're ownership rewards.

You're not a gambler. You're a business partner. And when the company wins, you don't just cheer—you get paid.

1. What Are Dividends, Really?

A dividend is a slice of the company's profit shared with shareholders.

- Usually paid quarterly, in cash or additional shares
- Can be fixed, variable, or growing over time

Translation:

You're not just hoping the stock goes up—you're earning while you wait.

If a stock pays a 3% annual dividend, and you own $10,000 worth, that's $300 a year in cash. If you reinvest it? That's compound growth—on autopilot.

2. Why Dividends Matter (More Than You Think)

Most people chase growth. But in the long run, dividends have been responsible for 40%–50% of total stock market returns.

Let that sink in.

Some of the world's greatest investors—Buffett, Bogle, Lynch—didn't obsess over price charts. They bought companies that:

◈ Had stable earnings

◈ Paid regular, growing dividends

◈ Reinvented profits back into the business

And they held them—for decades.

Dividend investing is a marathon.

But if you're consistent, it becomes the most powerful wealth engine in your portfolio.

3. The Three Kinds of Dividend Stocks

Here's how I categorize them inside Carbonado Capital:

A. Dividend Kings

- Companies that have raised dividends 50+ years in a row
- Example: Coca-Cola, Procter & Gamble, Johnson & Johnson
- These are your anchors—steady, boring, dependable.

B. Dividend Growers

- Companies that raise dividends consistently
- Often still growing revenue and expanding
- Example: Texas Instruments, Home Depot
- These offer income and growth—a beautiful balance.

C. High Yielders (Use Caution)

- These pay big dividends (often 5%+)
- But may carry risk—debt, market volatility, etc.
- Example: AT&T (past), real estate trusts, MLPs
- Vet them carefully—sometimes the yield is high for a reason.

◈ Tex Talks:

"If the yield looks too good to be true, it probably is. Don't get seduced by the number—study the business behind it."

4. Reinvestment: The Silent Multiplier

One of the smartest strategies in wealth-building is called a DRIP:

Dividend Reinvestment Plan.

Instead of pocketing your dividends, you use them to buy more shares. Automatically. Every quarter.

This does two things:

1. Increases your share count
2. Increases future dividends

And over time? That small drip becomes a flood of wealth.

Example:

- $10,000 invested in a 3% dividend stock, reinvested quarterly, could turn into $24,000+ in 20 years—even if the stock price never moved.

That's the power of compounding. And it requires no emotion—just consistency.

II: How to Identify Dividend Powerhouses

◈ Tex Talks:

"Anyone can find a stock that pays a dividend. I'm looking for the ones that never stop."

Not all dividend-paying stocks are created equal. Some are slow-burning dynamos with fortress balance sheets and decades of uninterrupted payouts. Others are traps—companies bleeding cash, overpromising yield, or clinging to dividends as a last-ditch effort to attract investors.

This section is about separating the wheat from the weeds. Here's how to spot the true dividend powerhouses—the ones that can fund your lifestyle and fuel your legacy.

1. The Dividend Scorecard

When evaluating a dividend stock, these are the categories I run it through:

A. Dividend Yield

- What it is: The percentage of the stock's price paid out annually as a dividend
- Why it matters: Too low? You're not getting paid. Too high? Might be unsustainable.
- Sweet spot: 2%–4% for growth + safety

Avoid 7%+ unless you've done deep risk analysis.

B. Payout Ratio

- What it is: % of earnings paid out as dividends
- Why it matters: Tells you if the company can afford its dividend

- Safe zone: < 60% for most sectors

High payout = risky if earnings drop. Low payout = room for future raises.

C. Dividend Growth History

- What it is: Years of consecutive dividend increases
- Why it matters: Proves consistency, shareholder loyalty, and financial strength

Look for 10+ years of uninterrupted growth. Bonus points for 25+.

D. Free Cash Flow (FCF)

- What it is: Cash left after expenses and investments
- Why it matters: Dividends are paid with cash—not earnings.

FCF is king. If it's shrinking, that dividend is in danger.

2. Red Flags to Watch For

Even seasoned investors get caught in dividend traps. Here are my top danger signs:

Red Flag	What It Signals
Rising payout ratio + flat earnings	Company might cut dividend soon
No dividend increases for 3+ years	Growth has stalled—or trouble is coming
Debt-fueled dividends	They are borrowing just to maintain appearances
Inconsistent free cash flow	Dividend is fragile and unreliable
Headline-only appeal	Just because Jim Cramer said it doesn't mean it's safe

◈ Tex Talks:

"If they gotta borrow to pay you, they're not blessing you—they're bluffing you."

3. Dividend Screening: The Carbonado Method

At Carbonado Capital, our dividend screen uses a strict filter:

Filter	Threshold
Dividend Yield	2.5%–4.5%
Payout Ratio	< 65%
Dividend Growth	≥ 10 years
FCF Coverage	Yes (FCF > Dividends paid)
Return on Equity	> 10%
Net Debt to EBITDA	< 2.5x

We run hundreds of companies through this lens quarterly. Only the top 5% make it to our shortlist.

Example:
PepsiCo (PEP) checked every box:

- 3% yield
- 48% payout ratio
- 50+ years dividend growth
- Bulletproof FCF
- Brand moat + global scale

That's what a dividend powerhouse looks like.

4. The Hidden Advantage: Downturn Performance

One reason dividend stocks matter?
They keep paying—even when markets crash.
During the 2008 financial crisis:

- Many tech and growth stocks cratered 50–80%.
- Dividend aristocrats held firm, many raised payouts.

Why? These companies have pricing power, stable demand, and loyal investors.

Owning them is like holding a steady-paying rental property—no matter what the real estate market says your house is worth today, the checks keep coming.

III: The DRIP Strategy – How Small Checks Build Big Wealth

⯑ Tex Talks:

"Dividends are nice. Reinvested dividends are a weapon. That's how I turned mailbox money into million-dollar muscle."

1. What Is a DRIP?

Dividend Reinvestment Plans (DRIPs) automatically reinvest your dividend payouts into additional shares of the same company—fractional or whole.

Think of it like compound interest for ownership.

- Instead of taking $20 and spending it, you use it to buy more shares.
- Next quarter? You get a dividend on those new shares too.
- Repeat that for 10, 20, 30 years?

Now you're not just getting paid. You're building equity on autopilot.

2. DRIP in Action: The Power of Snowballing

Let's break it down with a real example from one of our clients at Carbonado:

Client: Male, age 30, initial investment: $25,000

Stock: Johnson & Johnson (JNJ), ~2.8% yield

Strategy: DRIP, no withdrawals

Timeframe: 25 years

Result:

- Portfolio value: ~$140,000

- Dividends earned: ~$47,000
- Shares owned: Nearly doubled—without any new deposits

Key insight: Even in modest-growth stocks, reinvested dividends quietly multiply your stake.

> Without the DRIP, he'd still be holding $25K in principal plus maybe $30K in cash.
>
> With the DRIP, he's got a growing asset base and escalating dividend income.

---

3. How to Set It Up

- Most brokerages (Fidelity, Schwab, Merrill, etc.) allow you to opt into DRIPs with a toggle.
- You can select company-by-company.
- No fees, no taxes until you sell the shares.
- No effort. Just results.

◈ Tex Talks:
"The DRIP doesn't care about market noise. It doesn't panic sell. It just keeps buying—quietly, relentlessly, and without emotion."

Section IV: Dividend Aristocrats and How to Build Your Own

◈ Tex Talks:

"I don't chase royalty. I buy it. And in the market, the aristocrats don't wear crowns—they raise checks."

---

1. What Are Dividend Aristocrats?

These are elite companies in the S&P 500 that have:

- Paid—and increased—dividends every year for at least 25 consecutive years

They're not just stable. They're disciplined, shareholder-focused, and structurally sound. These companies have weathered:

- Dot-com bubble
- 9/11
- 2008 crash
- COVID-19 pandemic
- Inflationary waves
- Interest rate hikes

And they still kept cutting checks.

---

2. Examples of Dividend Aristocrats

Here are a few stalwarts:

Company	Sector	Consecutive Years Raised
Coca-Cola (KO)	Consumer Staples	61+ years
Procter & Gamble (PG)	Consumer Products	67+ years
McDonald's (MCD)	Restaurants	45+ years
Lowe's (LOW)	Home Improvement	50+ years
Chevron (CVX)	Energy	36+ years

These aren't just companies—they're financial fortresses.

---

3. Building Your Own Aristocrat Portfolio

You don't need 50 names. Start small, focused, and intentional.

Suggested approach:

- 40% in Dividend Kings (50+ years of raises)
- 30% in Aristocrats with strong balance sheets
- 20% in up-and-coming Dividend Growers
- 10% in high yielders (risk-managed)

Key metric to track:

> Dividend CAGR (Compound Annual Growth Rate) over 5–10 years

Look for companies raising dividends by at least 5% per year.

◈ Tex Talks:

"Don't just chase the current yield—study the dividend's trajectory. That's the growth curve that feeds generations."

Section V: The Retirement Engine – Living Off Dividends

◈ Tex Talks:

"In retirement, I don't sell assets—I harvest income. Dividends are my pension, but better."

---

1. The Math of a Dividend-Powered Retirement

Let's say you retire with a $1,000,000 portfolio.

Instead of selling shares, you've built a dividend machine that yields 4% annually.

Result:

You generate $40,000/year in income—without touching your principal.

> Markets down? You still get paid.
>
> Inflation creeping up? Your dividend growers raise payouts.
>
> Need more? Reinvest until you hit $60K or $80K annually.

This is the holy grail of financial independence:
Income without depletion.

---

2. Sequence of Returns Risk: The Silent Killer

One of the biggest threats to retirees is having to sell investments in a down market.

Dividend investors? Protected.

Because you don't have to sell shares. Your income keeps flowing, even when markets correct.

This stabilizes your retirement plan, protects longevity, and lowers emotional pressure to time the market.

---

3. Your Dividend Ladder Strategy

Build a dividend ladder that grows with you:

Age	Dividend Yield Target	Strategy
30s–40s	2–3%	Focus on dividend growth & DRIPs
50s	3–4%	Blend of growth and yield
60s+	4–5%	Focus on stability and income consistency

Don't just think about the current yield. Think about future income velocity. That's where real security lives.

◈ Tex Talks:

"If your portfolio doesn't pay you while you sleep, you'll be working until you die. Dividends change that math—permanently."

VI: Case Study – The $100K Dividend Portfolio

◈ Tex Talks:

"Don't ask how much a stock costs. Ask how much it pays you. That's the difference between a consumer and a capitalist."

The Goal

Build a dividend-paying portfolio with $100,000 that yields at least $4,000 a year, is diversified, and positioned for long-term growth. No trading. No selling. Just ownership that pays you back.

The Setup

Client Profile:

- Name: Rachel
- Age: 42
- Occupation: Mid-level HR director
- Risk Profile: Moderate
- Objective: Supplement future retirement with stable, growing dividend income

---

The Allocation

Company	Sector	Yield	Rationale	Allocation
Johnson & Johnson (JNJ)	Healthcare	2.9%	Blue-chip, 60-year dividend history	$15,000
Realty Income (O)	REIT	5.5%	Monthly payer, consistent REIT cash flow	$10,000
Chevron (CVX)	Energy	4.0%	Global energy infrastructure	$10,000
PepsiCo (PEP)	Consumer Staples	2.8%	Pricing power, global brand	$10,000
Main Street Capital (MAIN)	BDC	6.8%	High-yield, well-managed	$7,500
Microsoft (MSFT)	Tech	0.8%	Low yield, high dividend growth	$12,500
AT&T (T)	Telecom	6.7%	High income, turnaround play	$5,000
Procter & Gamble (PG)	Consumer Goods	2.5%	Recession-proof, steady growth	$10,000
Vanguard High Dividend ETF (VYM)	ETF	3.3%	Built-in diversification	$10,000

Company	Sector	Yield	Rationale	Allocation
Cash Reserve	N/A	0%	Flexibility for opportunities	$10,000

Projected Annual Income: $4,020

This portfolio generates just over 4% in dividends annually, with room for growth. Some positions (MSFT, JNJ, PG) are lower yield today but raise payouts aggressively, increasing Rachel's income every year.

Why It Works

- Diversification: From real estate (O) to tech (MSFT) to consumer staples (PG), this portfolio isn't relying on one industry.
- Dividend Growth: Even the lower-yield stocks are future income machines.
- Income Now, More Later: A blend of yield and appreciation means Rachel isn't sacrificing tomorrow for today.
- Monthly Income: Thanks to Realty Income and MAIN, Rachel sees cash flow every single month.

◈ Tex Talks:

"$100K isn't a lot in the stock market—unless you own it right. Then it becomes a printing press that never runs out of ink."

VII: Legacy Builder – Pastor James and the 5-Figure Passive Pipeline

◈ Tex Talks:

"You can preach stewardship all day long, but if your portfolio doesn't reflect the sermon, you're just passing the plate and not filling it."

The Man: Pastor James Whitfield

Houston, Texas.

Age 58.

Senior Pastor at a growing inner-city church.

Heart of gold. Voice like thunder. Finances? A quiet storm.

He'd spent three decades giving to others, tithing faithfully, building ministries, funding mission trips—but not building wealth for himself.

When he came to me, he said something that stuck with me like Texas heat in August:

> "Doc, I've built God's house for years. But I never built my own."

The Intervention: One Saturday, One Whiteboard, One Vision

We met in the church basement after a stewardship seminar I'd led.

He had $180,000 in retirement, sitting in a mix of underperforming mutual funds and money markets.

He wasn't broke.

But he was bleeding opportunity.

We sketched out a new plan right there—with a dry erase marker and a Kingdom mindset:

- Reallocate $150K into dividend growth stocks
- Keep $30K for emergencies and flexibility
- Focus on income, not just appreciation
- Build a pipeline that would fund both his family and his future church planting goals

---

The Portfolio

Here's the dividend pipeline we constructed:

Company	Sector	Yield	Allocation
Enterprise Products Partners (EPD)	Energy/MLP	7.2%	$25,000
AbbVie Inc. (ABBV)	Healthcare	3.6%	$25,000
McDonald's (MCD)	Consumer Discretionary	2.4%	$20,000
Kimberly-Clark (KMB)	Consumer Staples	3.8%	$15,000
Realty Income (O)	REIT	5.5%	$20,000
Vanguard Dividend Appreciation ETF (VIG)	ETF	2.2%	$25,000
Verizon (VZ)	Telecom	6.6%	$10,000
Microsoft (MSFT)	Tech	0.8%	$10,000

Annual Income: ~$6,700 (and rising)

Projected in 10 years: ~$10,000–12,000+ with reinvestment and growth

---

The Impact

That portfolio became his financial sermon.

- He taught monthly investment classes at the church
- He opened custodial Roth IRAs for his grandkids
- He donated his entire birthday to build a well in Ghana—funded solely from dividends

And when a congregant asked how he could afford to be so generous?

He smiled and said:

> "Because I stopped working for money. Now money works for me—and the Kingdom."

◈ Tex Talks:

"True wealth isn't selfish. It's structured. Pastor James didn't just tithe—he built a system that could tithe long after he's gone."

VIII: Action Plan – Build Your Own Dividend Empire

◈ Tex Talks:

"Don't chase income—engineer it. Dividends aren't gifts. They're your rightful cut as an owner. So act like one."

Step 1: Define Your Target

Before you buy anything, define what income means for you.

Ask yourself:

- How much annual income do I want my portfolio to generate?
- Am I investing for cash flow now, or growth that pays later?
- What's my monthly passive income target 5 years from today?

◈ Write it down. Bold and clear. Then reverse-engineer from there.

Step 2: Screen for Dividend Payers—The Right Way

Don't just Google "high dividend stocks." That's a trap. You want:

- Consistent payers (10+ year track records)
- Reasonable payout ratios (under 70% preferred)
- Dividend growth (rising payouts = rising income)
- Sector diversification (don't load up on just REITs or energy)

Use free tools like:

- Dividend.com
- SeekingAlpha (Dividend Scorecard)

- Finviz (Screener → Dividend Yield filter)

◈ Build a shortlist of 10–15 companies with solid fundamentals and dividends.

Step 3: Research Like a Capital Allocator

Pick three from your list and go deeper:

- Read their most recent 10-K
- Look at their dividend history on Nasdaq.com
- Check payout ratio, cash flow, and earnings trend

Ask yourself:

- Is this company positioned to keep paying—even in a recession?
- Is it growing, or just surviving?
- Would I be proud to own this business for the next decade?

◈ Make your first mock portfolio. No money yet—just theory and conviction.

Step 4: Open the Right Account

For tax efficiency, open:

- A Roth IRA (ideal for tax-free dividend compounding)
- A brokerage account (for larger, taxable investments)

- Consider DRIP (Dividend Reinvestment Plan) enrollment to compound without emotion

◈ Platforms: Fidelity, Schwab, Vanguard, M1 Finance

Step 5: Buy with a Long-Term Mindset

When ready to deploy real capital:

- Use limit orders, not market orders
- Don't try to "time the bottom"—focus on buying quality
- Start small and scale in
- Set a calendar reminder every quarter to review performance and dividends

◈ Treat each investment like buying a business, not playing a slot machine.

Step 6: Track and Tweak

Set up a simple spreadsheet or use free tools like:

- TrackYourDividends.com
- Personal Capital
- Sharesight

Track:

- Dividend income by company
- Yield on cost
- Portfolio diversification

- Dividend growth over time

◈ Celebrate milestones: First $100/month? That's rent on a cell phone bill.

First $1,000/year? That's a vacation. First $10,000? That's a financial pivot point.

The Big Tex Challenge:

Build a portfolio that generates $500/month in passive income within 3 years.

How?

- Target a blended yield of 4–5%
- Reinvest every dividend
- Invest a minimum of $1,000/month
- Cut the noise, trust the research, and think like an owner

◈ Tex Talks:

"Don't just survive this economy. Outlast it. Build an empire that prints checks while you sleep—and leaves a legacy while you lead."

CHAPTER 13: THE WEALTH MINDSET – From Consumer to Owner

Section I: The Mental Shift – From Scarcity to Sovereignty

◈ Tex Talks:

"You can't build wealth with a welfare mindset. Scarcity is a lie sold by systems that fear your independence. Own your mind—then own the rest."

Before you buy your first share or close your first deal, you've got to confront the first battlefield: your mind.

Most people aren't broke because of a lack of money.

They're broke because of a deficit in identity.

They've been raised on:

- "Don't get your hopes up"
- "Just be grateful you've got a job"
- "Rich folks are greedy"
- "Debt is just a part of life"

That's not financial wisdom—that's generational programming.

But here's what I've learned in boardrooms, in Wharton classrooms, and sitting on dirt floors in South Dallas:

> You cannot rise into ownership while still thinking like prey.

The wealthy don't ask, "Can I afford this?"
They ask, "Should I own this?"
They don't fear risk.
They manage it, hedge it, and leverage it.
They don't spend to signal status.
They invest to secure sovereignty.
So if you're ready to cross over, burn this into your spirit:
◈ You are not a beggar. You are a builder.
◈ You are not a borrower. You are a bank.
◈ You are not a consumer. You are a creator.
Scarcity says: Survive.
Sovereignty says: Scale.

Section II: The Language of Ownership – What the Wealthy Think That Others Don't

◈ Tex Talks:

"Wealthy people speak in balance sheets. Everyone else talks in receipts. If you want to own the game, learn the language."

Wealth has a language. And most of America is financially illiterate—not because they're dumb, but because they were never taught the dialect of power.

Let's decode the translation:

Poor/Middle Class Say...	**Owners Think...**
"That's expensive."	"What's the ROI?"
"I need a raise."	"I need equity."
"I want to retire."	"I want passive income."
"I hope they pick me."	"I'm picking myself."
"Money is the root of all evil."	"Ignorance is."

You were taught how to earn a paycheck, not how to think like an investor. You were told to avoid debt but never taught how the wealthy use debt as leverage. You were raised to work for money but never shown how money can be trained to work for you.

I remember a young man once asked me, "Dr. Thomas, how do rich people stay rich?"

My answer was simple:

> "They speak a different language. And the IRS listens."

They understand depreciation, asset protection, tax deferral, and liquidity events.

They form trusts while you're focused on credit scores.

They buy assets before they buy Jordans.

It's not about intelligence—it's about exposure.

You don't need to be a genius to be wealthy.

You just need to unlearn the lies and start thinking like an owner.

Section III: The Consumer Trap – How

the System Is Built to Keep You Powerless

◈ Tex Talks:

"The system doesn't want you free. It wants you financing your own chains—30 years at 4.5% interest."

Let's not sugarcoat this: The American economy thrives on your financial ignorance.

It's not just "bad decisions." It's designed dependence.

Every advertisement, every credit offer, every flashy subscription is engineered to do one thing:

> Keep you buying what someone else owns.

Here's how the trap works:

1. You earn money.
2. You're taught to spend it immediately (consumerism).
3. You rack up debt to fund your lifestyle (credit cards, auto loans, student loans).
4. You become enslaved to payments and dependent on income.
5. You never build assets—just liabilities and regret.
6. The rich? They collect the interest.

It's a rigged loop. A treadmill disguised as a dream.

That's why every time you get a raise, the ads get louder.

That's why you're encouraged to "treat yourself" every payday instead of buying a slice of the very company that just sold you the sneakers.

You're not just a consumer. You're a commodity.

Your time. Your data. Your attention. Your labor.

They've made a market out of your life—and you're trading it for things that lose value the moment you walk out the store.

But not anymore.

You're flipping the script.

You're breaking the loop.

You're crossing the line—from consumer to owner.

◈ Tex Talks:

"Ownership is the antidote to economic slavery. The second you stop renting your lifestyle and start owning your future, the system starts to lose its grip."

Section IV: Ownership in Action – Case Studies from the Field

◈ Tex Talks:

"Theory dies in the field. Show me the receipts. Show me the generational shift. Show me what ownership looks like in real life."

Yolanda – The First-Timer Turned Franchise Queen

Yolanda was a night-shift nurse. Single mom. No inheritance. No Ivy League degree.

What she did have? An open seat at one of my "Financials for First-Timers" workshops and a fire in her spirit.

She didn't ask about crypto. She asked about McDonald's.

She read their 10-K, spotted the 60% franchise margin, and realized:

> "The Big Mac is the bait. The business is real estate and royalties."

Fast-forward three years:

- Bought her first rental using a HELOC and Section 8 strategy
- Bought stock in McDonald's, then Starbucks, then Realty Income Corp
- Launched a home healthcare business in Houston
- Today? $281K portfolio, owns 3 doors, daughter at Vanderbilt. Debt-free.

She became a quiet millionaire, not by playing the lottery—but by owning what she once consumed.

Jamal – From Prison Hustler to Investment Advisor

Jamal served 9 years for trafficking. In that time, he read every book I recommended, front to back.

He started paper trading with commissary math, simulating ETF positions with notebook entries and weekly Barron's stats.

His biggest lesson?

> "If I can master risk from a 6x9 cell with no Wi-Fi, I can dominate it with a Bloomberg terminal."

He walked out of prison with an investment certification, got hired at a boutique firm in Atlanta, and now manages over $7 million AUM.

From concrete walls to capital management. That's ownership.

The Thomas Family Ranch – Legacy in Motion

Your own story, Big Tex, is proof. You didn't just inherit a ranch—you turned it into a holding company.

You didn't stop at cattle—you expanded into:

- Alternative energy (wind leases on the land)
- Real estate development (ranch-to-resort transitions)
- Branding initiatives (Heated Armor, Global Hair 4U)

This isn't about land. It's about using what you own to scale what you believe in.

You taught your children the ownership mindset early. Kylie runs the publishing house. Kendall's learning the books. The legacy isn't money—it's mentality.

That's what this book delivers.

Section V: Faith and Finance – Why Stewardship Requires Strategy

� Tex Talks:

"God doesn't call us to be broke. He calls us to be wise. The harvest is there—but only for those who sow in strategy and reap with stewardship."

Let's set the record straight:

Faith isn't an excuse for financial ignorance.

The Bible doesn't glorify poverty—it warns against arrogance, idolatry, and greed. But stewardship? That's a divine mandate.

> "To whom much is given, much will be required."
> – Luke 12:48

And that includes knowledge.

You've been entrusted with gifts. Talent. Vision. Discipline.

But if you're burying your financial potential under shame, fear, or laziness—don't call that humility. That's disobedience.

Wealth isn't just about your lifestyle.

It's about your impact.

- Can you fund the vision?
- Can you rescue someone else's dream?
- Can you bless without asking for a GoFundMe?

That's not greed. That's gospel.

The early church? Asset-based. Landowners sold property to care for others.

Joseph in Egypt? Managed surplus for a nation.

Solomon? Operated an economic empire with international trade.

You're not just called to believe. You're called to build.

◈ Build margin.

◈ Build enterprise.

◈ Build legacy.

Because money in the hands of the righteous is a force hell can't contain.

Section VI: The Ownership Creed – Living Above the Line

◈ Tex Talks:

"Some folks live below the line: paycheck to paycheck, dream to disaster. Owners live above the line—where strategy beats survival."

What separates owners from everyone else? Mindset and method.

I teach it this way:

Below the Line	**Above the Line**
Reacts to bills	Plans with budgets
Chases trends	Builds thesis-driven portfolios
Lives on credit	Builds credit intentionally
Sells in fear	Buys with conviction
Pays interest	Earns interest

Living above the line doesn't mean you're perfect. It means you have a plan—and you work the plan.

You don't need millions to start thinking like an owner.

You need:

- A clear reason
- A defined number
- A system of accountability
- And a willingness to delay what's easy for what's eternal

Here's the creed:

> "I don't chase. I build. I don't beg. I own. I don't fear money. I govern it."

When you internalize that, your habits change.
Your standards rise.
Your circle shifts.
And your ceiling becomes your floor.
That's the power of ownership. That's what we do.

Section VII: Action Plan – Flip the Switch, Start the Climb

◈ Tex Talks:

"Talk is cheap. Execution is equity. If you're not willing to move your feet, don't waste your breath. Let's build."

This is Your Wake-Up Call.

You've read about budgets, investing, risk, and ownership.

But none of it matters until you choose to think differently.

This isn't about reading another book or watching another video.

This is about shifting your identity from consumer to owner, once and for all.

◈ Step One: Write Your Ownership Statement

Take a pen and write this—by hand:

> "I will no longer live below the line.
>
> I am not just a spender, a borrower, or a worker.
>
> I am an investor. I am a builder. I am an owner.
>
> I will control what I can, invest what I earn, and leave more than I take."

Sign it. Date it. Tape it above your workspace. Ownership begins with a declaration.

◈ Step Two: Build Your First Ownership Asset

Pick one of the following and take action within the next 48 hours:

- Stock ownership: Open an account and buy one share of a company you understand.
- Small business: Register your LLC. Even if it's just an idea—formalize it.
- Digital asset: Buy your personal domain name

(e.g., YourName.com) and start building your platform.

- Intellectual property: Write and self-publish a short eBook or course. Ownership isn't always physical.

This is about planting your first flag. Not waiting for permission. Not asking anyone to validate you.

◈ Step Three: Audit Your Circle

Ownership is not just about assets—it's about alignment.

Ask:

- Who in my life encourages financial responsibility?
- Who dismisses my goals or ridicules ambition?
- Who teaches me how to invest, build, and multiply?

Start closing emotional accounts with people who only drain. You can't build wealth in a room full of scarcity thinkers.

◈ Step Four: Join the 1% Club — In Mindset

Not in net worth—yet.

But in thinking, you can join the top 1% starting now.

That means:

- You know your number

- You track your net worth monthly
- You read financial statements regularly
- You study capital flows, not celebrity gossip
- You act like a trustee of future wealth—not a slave to the moment

This mindset isn't reserved for billionaires. It's reserved for the bold.

◈ Step Five: Teach Someone Else

Ownership multiplies when it's shared.

If you've made it this far in the book, you're already ahead of 90% of the population.

Now share the blueprint.

- Teach your kids the difference between assets and liabilities.
- Talk to your spouse about net worth, not just bills.
- Lead a financial literacy workshop.
- Mentor someone coming out of prison or poverty.

Ownership isn't just about you. It's about becoming a living blueprint for someone else's breakthrough.

◈ Tex Talks (Final Word of the Chapter):

"You don't need permission. You don't need a miracle. You need a decision. Ownership begins when you stop outsourcing your power. The climb starts now."

CHAPTER 14: THE CREDIT GAME – Leveraging Debt Without Getting Played

⟐ Tex Talks:

"Credit isn't evil. It's just dangerous in the hands of amateurs. The same gasoline that fuels a Bentley can also burn down a barn."

Section I: Credit is a Tool—Not a Trophy

Credit isn't money. It's permission to use someone else's.

That permission can be leveraged into power—or into poverty.

Let's break it down clearly:

- Credit is a tool.
- Tools require skill.
- Skill requires discipline.

Too many folks treat credit like a status symbol—bragging about high limits while drowning in minimum payments. That's not power. That's bondage in a business suit.

Real credit mastery comes when you stop chasing what you can get and start using credit to get what you can build.

> You don't swipe for sneakers. You swipe for strategies.

High credit isn't about vanity—it's about velocity:

- Velocity of business capital.
- Velocity of opportunity.
- Velocity of scaled ownership.

If you treat credit like cash, you'll go broke.
If you treat it like a lever, you can move empires.

Section II: Understanding How Credit Actually Works

🔎 Tex Talks:

"If you don't know how they score you, you don't know how they control you."

Your credit score isn't a mystery. It's a formula. And once you understand it, you stop fearing it.

Here's how it breaks down:

Factor	Weight	What It Means
Payment History	35%	Do you pay on time, every time? This is non-negotiable.
Credit Utilization	30%	How much of your limit are you using? Keep it under 10%, not just 30%.
Credit Age	15%	How long have you had your accounts? Old cards are gold—don't close them.
Credit Mix	10%	Do you have different types? (Credit cards, loans, etc.) Shows depth.
New Credit Inquiries	10%	Too many applications = risk. Protect your score like your Social.

Let's call this what it is: a game.

And in every game, the house has rules. You're either a pawn—or a player who knows how to bend those rules to win legally.

The Big Tex Credit Principle: Leverage Without Leash

You only use credit:

- When you already have a cash plan behind it
- When the ROI beats the interest
- When you control the terms—not the lender

You're not borrowing for a lifestyle.

You're borrowing to scale your ownership, accelerate income, or preserve liquidity.

No plan? No purchase.

Section III: Good Debt vs. Bad Debt – Know the Difference

🔶 Tex Talks:

"Debt ain't good or bad. It's either productive or parasitic. One builds your empire. The other eats it alive."

Let's remove the shame from the word "debt" and inject some strategy.

Good Debt is debt that pays you back—with interest.

Bad Debt is debt that costs you sleep, peace, and freedom.

Here's the breakdown:

Good Debt	Why It's Strategic
Real estate mortgage on a cash-flowing property	Builds equity, provides rental income, appreciates over time
Business line of credit used for inventory expansion	Increases revenue-generating capacity
Student loan (strategically chosen field)	Raises income potential significantly when ROI is clear and planned
Low-interest leverage for stock/investment purchase	When backed by due diligence and stop-loss strategies

Bad Debt is what you incur for instant gratification or ego-driven consumption:

- Maxed-out credit cards for luxury goods

- Car notes on depreciating vehicles you can't afford
- Payday loans or high-interest consumer financing
- "Buy Now, Pay Later" traps with no exit strategy

You weren't called to be a slave to interest.

You were called to own the gates. That begins with drawing a hard line between leverage and liability.

Section IV: Credit as Capital – Using Other People's Money Like a Pro

◈ Tex Talks:

"Banks lend to the bold—if you speak their language. Learn it, and their vaults swing open."

Most people think of credit as a lifeline.

The wealthy think of it as capital.

Let's be clear: Credit is OPM—Other People's Money. And if you know how to use it right, it becomes a fuel source for ownership.

You don't take out credit because you're desperate. You take it because you're strategic.

◈ Use Credit To:

- Launch a business with clear revenue projections
- Acquire appreciating assets (real estate, inventory, equity stakes)
- Bridge temporary cash flow gaps in a proven operation
- Invest in tools, certifications, or infrastructure that

have a measurable return

But you only borrow when:

- The ROI is greater than the APR
- The terms are negotiable
- The payoff plan is pre-written

If you're using a credit card to survive, stop. That's financial quicksand.

If you're using a business line of credit to scale proven revenue, proceed—with surgical precision.

At Carbonado, we used bank capital not for comfort, but for conquest. We didn't ask what we could "afford"—we asked what would multiply.

Section V: Credit Repair vs. Credit Strategy – Don't Just Fix It, Weaponize It

◈ Tex Talks:

"A 750 credit score means nothing if you don't know what to do with it. A loaded gun in the hands of a child is just as dangerous as debt in the hands of the untrained."

Most people treat credit repair like it's a finish line. It's not.

Fixing your credit is just getting your name back in the game.

Strategizing your credit is how you start playing to win.

Here's the difference:

Credit Repair	**Credit Strategy**
Disputing negative items	Structuring credit usage for optimal scoring
Paying collections or negotiating settlements	Leveraging tradelines to boost score & age
Securing secured cards to build history	Getting Tier 1 cards with business-friendly terms
Watching your score	Building a financial profile that unlocks opportunity

The Goal is Not a Score. The Goal is Leverage.

Here's what we teach at Carbonado:

- Never just aim to get approved.

Aim to get pre-approved, pre-qualified, and negotiated.

- Never max out a line.

Keep it light, paid on time, and let your profile look like a quiet millionaire.

- Never use credit emotionally.

Use it for ownership, expansion, and legacy.

A perfect credit score in the hands of someone with no plan is just a shiny liability.

But in your hands? It's a bulletproof business tool.

Section VI: Credit and Identity – Building a Profile That Commands Respect

◈ Tex Talks:

"Credit is your digital reputation. Protect it like your name, build it like your brand."

Here's the truth the system won't tell you: You are being judged.

Every time you swipe, apply, borrow, or delay—your digital fingerprint is being analyzed.

That fingerprint is your financial identity—and it's just as real as your Social Security number.

So ask yourself:

- Does your credit profile look like a consumer or a controller?
- Are you being profiled as risky, reliable, or respected?

This isn't about fake flexing. It's about curating a profile that reflects your values, your discipline, and your direction.

Build Like a Boss:

- Keep old accounts open. History = power.
- Use multiple forms of credit strategically. Not just cards—auto, business, lines of credit.

- Keep utilization low, but activity consistent. Be visible without being volatile.
- Freeze your credit when not using it. Prevent identity theft. This is your castle—guard it.
- Monitor your reports monthly. If a lender is watching you, you better be watching yourself.

Your name deserves to be associated with excellence, stability, and vision. Make your credit reflect that.

This isn't just about FICO. It's about financial posture.

Section VII: Action Plan – Build Credit Power the Big Tex Way

◈ Tex Talks:

"Credit isn't something you build when you need it. It's something you sharpen like a blade—so when the time comes, you cut through the noise and claim your territory."

This isn't about theory. It's about execution.

And I don't care if you're rebuilding from scratch or fine-tuning a 780 score—every reader can level up today.

Let's put the plan in motion:

◈

Step 1: Pull Your Full Credit Report

- Go to annualcreditreport.com[1]

1. https://www.annualcreditreport.com

- Pull reports from Experian, Equifax, and TransUnion
- Look for:
    - Errors or outdated accounts
    - Late payments
    - Charged-off accounts
    - Duplicate debt listings

◈ Tex Truth:
"You can't fix what you don't face. First step to ownership is oversight."

◈

Step 2: Create a Repair Strategy

- Dispute all errors through the bureaus (online or by mail)
- Negotiate any old collections—get a "pay for delete" in writing
- Pay down utilization to under 10% on all active cards
- Automate payments to avoid late marks ever again

If you need help, hire a pro. Not a hustler. A licensed, proven credit specialist.

◈

Step 3: Establish New Tradelines Wisely

- Open a secured card if you're rebuilding

- Ask existing creditors for limit increases (without a hard pull)
- Get added as an authorized user on a seasoned, clean account
- Use the "3 Card Rule":
    - 1 primary credit card
    - 1 gas/store card
    - 1 business or travel card

(All paid in full monthly)

◈

Step 4: Leverage Credit for Ownership

Once your credit profile is healthy:

- Apply for business credit lines tied to your LLC, not your name
- Use 0% APR intro offers strategically (short-term flips or investments)
- Use revolving credit only to buy things that produce cash flow or scale income
- Track your credit utilization, score changes, and report updates monthly

◈ Tex Reminder:

"Every swipe writes a story. Make sure yours ends in equity, not excuses."

◈

Step 5: Teach Someone Else

Because real wealth isn't just personal—it's generational.

- Teach your kids, mentees, or cellmates how credit works
- Show someone how to check their report
- Pass down the principle: Debt is either a chain or a key. You choose.

Big Tex Credit Challenge:

Within 30 days:

- Pull all 3 reports
- Eliminate 2 negative items
- Raise at least 1 limit
- Teach 1 person the credit game

Then email your progress to: BigTex@CarbonadoCapital.com.

⍰ Tex Talks:

"They built a system to measure your worth with numbers. I built a system to make those numbers bow to mine."

CHAPTER 15: REAL ESTATE – Owning Dirt, Building Dynasties

I. Why Real Estate Still Reigns: The King of All Asset Classes

◈ Tex Talks:

"The stock market builds portfolios. Real estate builds dynasties."

Let the pundits argue. Crypto comes and goes. Tech stocks rise and fall. But land? Land is eternal.

Even in volatile economies, real estate remains the cornerstone of generational wealth. Not because it's sexy. But because it's stable, strategic, and tangible. The wealthy don't just buy homes—they accumulate territory.

Let me be clear:

- Every millionaire I've ever sat across owned property.
- Every billionaire I've ever studied owned land.

Why? Because real estate:

- Pays you monthly (rents, leases, passive income)
- Appreciates steadily over time
- Comes with major tax advantages (depreciation, 1031 exchanges)

- Lets you use leverage (OPM) to grow wealth with limited cash
- Provides control over your asset (unlike stocks)

And here's the Big Tex kicker:

You don't need millions to start. You just need knowledge, guts, and the right deal.

II. The Four Paths to Real Estate Wealth

◈ Tex Talks:

"Don't wait to buy land. Buy land, and wait."

Real estate isn't one lane—it's a four-lane highway. Each lane builds wealth differently.

1. Rental Properties – Buy & Hold

- Long-term passive income
- Appreciation over time
- Can be residential (single-family, duplex) or commercial (retail, office)
- Managed by you or property managers

Best for investors who want monthly income and long-term growth

---

2. Flipping – Buy Low, Renovate, Sell High

- Short-term capital gains
- Requires renovation skills or contractor relationships
- Higher risk, higher reward
- Timing and comps matter

Best for skilled, hands-on investors with access to capital and renovation insight

---

3. Wholesaling – Find Deals, Sell Contracts

- No property ownership required
- Find motivated sellers, assign contracts to investors
- Requires hustle, negotiation, and a strong buyers list

Best for low-capital beginners who can network and move fast

---

4. Land Investing – Dirt Deals and Development

- Raw land, rezoning plays, agricultural flips
- Often overlooked, highly profitable
- Buy and hold or flip to developers

Best for visionaries who can wait and understand zoning laws and growth trends

---

You don't have to do all four. You just need to master one.

III. My First Property Deal: The One That Changed Everything

◈ Tex Talks:

"I didn't grow up owning land. But the first time I held a deed with my name on it, something shifted I stopped renting anything, including my mentality."

Let me take you back.

I was fresh out of grad school, full of ambition, and broke in the traditional sense—but rich in strategy. While most of my peers were buying cars and condos, I saw opportunity in the overlooked.

It was a 3-bedroom foreclosure in South Dallas, beat-up but solid bones.

- Purchase price: $42,000
- Rehab budget: $18,000
- Total all-in: $60,000
- After-repair value (ARV): $95,000
- Monthly rent: $1,200

I didn't flip it. I held it.

Because this was my first passive income stream. And the lesson it taught me?

> "Equity doesn't scream. It whispers."

I didn't brag about that property. I just collected the checks, paid down the mortgage, and reinvested.

That one house became three. Those three became twelve. And over time, they gave me the freedom to walk away from bad deals, bad people, and bad systems.

It's not about the house. It's about what the house can unlock.

Section IV: No Money Down? No Problem — Creative Financing Explained

🔶 Tex Talks:

"Banks open doors for the wealthy. The rest have to learn to build our own damn keys."

The biggest lie in real estate?

"You need money to make money."

Wrong. You need leverage, relationships, and creative tools. That's how wealth starts from nothing.

Let me show you the same financing strategies I used—and still teach.

---

1. Seller Financing

The seller acts as the bank. You agree to a down payment and monthly terms directly with them.

- Great for off-market or distressed deals
- Requires trust and negotiation

- No banks, no red tape

⟐ Best for beginners who find motivated sellers

---

2. Hard Money Loans

Short-term, high-interest loans based on the property's value—not your credit score.

- Fast approvals
- Used for flips and fast closes
- Must have an exit strategy

⟐ Best for experienced investors with a clear rehab-to-sale plan

---

3. Subject-To Financing

You take over the seller's existing mortgage "subject to" the current loan terms. They stay on the loan; you get the deed.

- No credit pull
- Keeps existing low interest rate
- Must be managed carefully to avoid default

⟐ Best for strategic investors in rising rate environments

---

4. Partnerships & Syndications

Bring in capital partners or pool investor money to do bigger deals.

- You bring the deal, they bring the dollars
- Split equity or cash flow
- Use operating agreements to protect all sides

◈ Best for networkers and visionaries with strong deal flow

---

5. Business Credit & Lines of Credit

Use business credit or HELOCs (Home Equity Lines of Credit) to acquire property or cover rehabs.

- Less risk to personal credit
- Great for BRRRR (Buy, Rehab, Rent, Refinance, Repeat) strategy
- Requires excellent planning

◈ Best for disciplined investors with cash flow projections

Real estate doesn't require cash—it requires confidence and a calculated plan.

And confidence comes from knowing your tools.

Section V: The Tax Code Loves Landowners — Use It

◈ Tex Talks:

"The rich don't dodge taxes—they study the playbook. Real estate is the playbook."

Here's the secret the IRS won't post on Instagram:

> Real estate is the most tax-advantaged asset in America.

Own property, and you unlock an entire side of the tax code built to reward builders.

Here's how:

---

1. Depreciation

The IRS lets you deduct part of your property's value every year—as if it's losing value—even while it appreciates.

- Residential: 27.5 years
- Commercial: 39 years
- Real-world result? Paper losses on appreciating assets

---

2. Mortgage Interest Deductions

Deduct interest paid on loans used to acquire or improve rental property. The bigger the debt, the bigger the write-off.

---

3. 1031 Exchange

Sell a property, reinvest the profits in a "like-kind" property, and defer capital gains taxes.

- Key to building an empire tax-deferred
- Can roll profits forward for decades

---

4. Repairs and Improvements

Write off every dollar spent improving the property. New roof? Tax deductible. New water heater? Same.

---

5. Cost Segregation

Accelerate depreciation by breaking out parts of the property (carpet, fixtures, etc.)

Major upfront savings—especially powerful for high-income investors.

◈ Tex Reminder:

"Every deduction is a dollar back in your empire. If you're paying full price on taxes, you're not a player. You're a pawn."

Section VI: Big Tex's Blueprint — How to Start From Anywhere

◈ Tex Talks:

"Don't tell me where you're from. Tell me what you're willing to learn."

I've mentored:

- A single mom in Baltimore who built a duplex portfolio using FHA loans
- A formerly incarcerated brother in Missouri who flipped three houses before his probation ended
- A Texas schoolteacher who bought land with

inheritance money and is now developing short-term rentals

Real estate isn't about background—it's about boldness.

Here's your starting point:

1. Get Educated
    - Read Rich Dad Poor Dad, The Millionaire Real Estate Investor, and actual zoning laws in your city
    - Listen to BiggerPockets, Meet Kevin, or real-deal mentors with receipts
2. Pick a Lane
    - Are you a cash-flow hunter? Start with small rentals.
    - Are you aggressive? Consider flips or wholesaling.
    - Do you have time but no money? Master deal finding.
3. Build Your Power Circle
    - Realtor
    - Contractor
    - Inspector
    - Lender
    - Insurance agent
    - Mentor or partner
    - Title company
4. Take the First Shot
    - Run comps

- Analyze a deal
- Make an offer
- Close one. Then do another.

You don't need to own 100 doors to win. You just need to own one to start playing.

◈ Tex Final Word:

"Land ownership is political. Economic. Spiritual. Take back your square foot, and you take back your power."

Section VII: The Real Estate Action Plan – Your First 90 Days

◈ Tex Talks:

"If you don't put this chapter into motion, it's just paper. If you do, it's a deed."

Let's go from dreaming about real estate to owning it.

Here's the 90-day blueprint. Tailored for beginners, built for boldness.

Week 1–2: Education and Exposure

- Read Rich Dad Poor Dad and The Book on Rental Property Investing (Brandon Turner)
- Watch free videos from BiggerPockets, Ryan Pineda, or Tex-approved mentors

- Follow 3 local real estate Facebook groups and attend 1 local meet-up (in person or Zoom)
- Start building a real estate vocabulary: comps, ARV, cap rate, LTV, NOI, wholesaling

---

Week 3–4: Market Research

- Choose one zip code in your area
- Track:
  - Listing prices
  - Rental rates
  - Days on market
  - Price reductions
- Identify:
  - 3 potential flip properties
  - 3 potential rentals
  - 1 off-market deal (Craigslist, driving for dollars, or agent whisper)

Week 5–6: Build Your Power Team

- Interview 3 realtors
- Meet with a lender or hard money source
- Call at least 1 title company and ask about investor-friendly closings
- Contact an insurance agent who specializes in rental property
- Line up a contractor or home inspector for future

walkthroughs

◈ Tex Reminder:

"If you don't build your circle now, you'll choke when the opportunity comes. This game ain't solo."

Week 7–8: Deal Analysis and Practice Offers

- Run numbers on at least 10 properties:
    - Purchase price
    - Rehab estimate
    - After-Repair Value (ARV)
    - Estimated cash flow
- Use deal calculators (or spreadsheets) to determine if it's a go/no-go
- Make at least 1 written offer (even if it's rejected—you need reps)

Week 9–12: Go All In

- Lock in financing
- Make your strongest offer yet
- If accepted: close, rehab, rent, or flip
- If not accepted: keep analyzing and offering

Momentum is built through motion.

◈ Bonus Assignments:

- Set your real estate goal:

"I will own my first cash-flowing property by ___________."

- Share it publicly with your accountability partner
- Email it to BigTex@CarbonadoCapital.com for real feedback

◈ Tex Closer:

"The first deal is the scariest. It's also the one that changes everything. Don't wait for confidence—build it through action."

CHAPTER 16: ENTREPRENEURSHIP — FROM HUSTLE TO HOLDINGS

◈ Tex Talks:

"Owning a business isn't about a storefront. It's about creating something the world pays you for — even while you sleep."

I. The Entrepreneur's Mindset: Not a Side Hustle — A Sovereign Identity

Entrepreneurship is not a gig. It's not about "being your own boss" because you hate managers. It's a mindset — and in my world, it's a strategic asset class.

It's the difference between asking, "What do I get paid to do?" and asking, "How do I build something that prints value?"

The broke man asks, "Who will hire me?"

The wealthy man asks, "What problems can I solve at scale?"

You don't get rich from trading time. You get rich from building systems. From owning the business — not working inside one.

That's the transition: from employee to enterprise. From hustler to holding company.

II. My First Real Business: Kiss My Grass Landscaping

◈ Tex Talks:

"Entrepreneurship didn't start for me in a boardroom. It started with a lawnmower and a clipboard at age twelve."

My first real business wasn't some side hustle. It wasn't a lemonade stand. It was Kiss My Grass Landscaping, and I launched it before I hit my teenage years.

At twelve, I wasn't looking for pocket change—I was looking for contracts. While other kids were inside playing video games, I was out knocking on doors, negotiating seasonal rates, and walking properties with a notepad and a vision. I didn't just cut lawns—I built a brand.

And like any smart CEO, I didn't do all the work myself.

- I hired my friends, paid them fairly, and scheduled the jobs.
- I handled the billing, client retention, and customer service.
- I built out weekend crews, managed multiple properties, and kept a tight eye on cash flow.

By the time I was ready for college, I had sold the company for six figures.

That's not an exaggeration. That's a blueprint.

> I didn't wait for permission to become a businessman. I created opportunity, systemized labor, and exited with profit. That's entrepreneurship.

This wasn't a hobby. This was an early education in leadership, leverage, and liquidity. It taught me how to:

- Identify recurring problems (overgrown lawns, unreliable yard guys)
- Offer a reliable, affordable, and premium service
- Scale it beyond myself through smart delegation

Long before I walked into Wharton or closed deals in the boardroom, I had already proven one thing: I could build, scale, and sell.

◈ Tex Reminder:

"You don't need an MBA to start a business. But when you do it right, you might end up teaching MBAs how it's done."

III. Business Is the New Plantation — So Be the Landowner

◈ Tex Talks:

"They'll sell you wages. I sell you freedom. Because ownership ain't optional—it's oxygen."

Let's be blunt:

Most Americans work for someone else's dream.

They clock in, produce, clock out, and hope for a 3% raise.

That's not wealth — that's captivity with benefits.

Starting your own business is a political act.

It says: "I won't depend on the system to feed me."

It says: "I'll build my own table — and pass it to my kids."

IV. Types of Business Models That Build Wealth

All businesses are not created equal. Here's a breakdown of models that scale, systemize, and multiply wealth.

Business Model	**Why It Wins**	**Example**
Service-Based	Low startup cost, skills-based	Consulting, cleaning, coaching
Product-Based (eComm)	Scales with ads & logistics	Shopify, Amazon FBA
Subscription (Recurring Revenue)	Predictable income, high valuation	SaaS, box delivery
Franchise Model	Rapid duplication, brand equity	Mobile barbershop, tutoring
Holding Company	Acquires or builds businesses	Thomas & Thomas Holdings

◈ Tex Reminder:

"If your business needs you 24/7 to survive, it's a job in disguise. Build systems, not shackles."

V. Building the Machine: Systems, SOPs, and Staff

Entrepreneurs burn out not from work — but from trying to do everything.

The transition from self-employed to CEO happens the moment you build:

- Standard Operating Procedures (SOPs)

  Write down how every task is done. Automate what you can.

- Staffing Smart

  Hire people better than you at specific roles. Pay well. Hold accountable.

- Sales Systems

  Your business is not about your product. It's about how consistently you acquire and keep customers.

If you don't build a machine, you are the machine. And machines break.

VI. The Legal & Financial Structure That Protects the Empire

You can't build wealth on shaky ground. Your business needs a legal and financial backbone:

- LLC or S-Corp → Protects personal assets
- Business Bank Account → Clean books = scalable business
- Accounting Software → QuickBooks, Wave, Xero
- Bookkeeper + CPA → Required. Not optional.
- Contracts → No handshakes. Use NDAs, service agreements, vendor contracts.

⍰ Tex Talks:

"They'll tell you to hustle. I'll tell you to protect your hustle."

VII. The Entrepreneur's Tax Advantage

Entrepreneurs don't just earn more — they keep more.

Tax Benefit	What It Means
Business Deductions	Meals, travel, phone, home office — all write-offs if tied to business
Depreciation on Assets	Vehicles, equipment, even office furniture = tax shields
Health Insurance Deductions	Deduct your premiums if self-employed
Retirement Accounts	SEP IRA, Solo 401(k) — higher contribution limits
Income Splitting	Pay your spouse or kids to reduce household taxes

⟐ Tex Reminder:

"You're not just building a business — you're building a tax strategy."

VIII. The Three Stages of Business Maturity

Every business evolves. Here's where you are—and where you're headed.

1. Survival Stage
    - You do everything
    - Cash flow is tight
    - Focus: Sales + delivery
2. Stability Stage
    - You have help
    - Cash flow is consistent
    - Focus: Systems + delegation

3. Scale Stage
   - You lead, not manage
   - Revenue multiplies
   - Focus: Expansion + exits

The key is to know where you are—and plan for where you're going.

IX. Legacy Builder Case Study: Carlos, the Hustler Turned Holding Company CEO

Carlos was slinging shirts out of his trunk in Houston. $20 tees. No website. No plan.

He joined one of my seminars, took notes like his life depended on it. He applied everything:

- Registered an LLC
- Opened a Stripe account
- Partnered with a printer
- Started drop shipping
- Built a Shopify store
- Automated fulfillment
- Scaled with Instagram ads

Today? He owns four brands, a warehouse, and a team of 12.

His latest investment? A barbershop he's turning into a franchise.

Net revenue last year: $1.3 million.

From hustle to holdings.

🔶 Tex Tribute:

"Carlos didn't just change his income. He changed his identity."

X. Action Challenge: Start, Structure, Scale

Do This Now:

1. Choose a Business Idea
    - What problem do you solve?
    - Who needs it most?
    - What are they already paying for?
2. Name It and Form It
    - Go to your Secretary of State's website
    - Register an LLC or DBA
    - Open a business bank account
3. Design the First Offer
    - What's the product/service?
    - How will you price it?
    - What makes it different?
4. Launch and Learn
    - Tell 10 people
    - Make your first sale
    - Get feedback
    - Tweak, grow, repeat
5. Email me — BigTex@CarbonadoCapital.com
    - Subject: "My Business, Day 1"
    - Tell me what you're building.

- My team shares them all with me.

◈ Tex Final Word:

"Business is the final frontier of freedom. Build one, or work for one. That's the choice. And you've already made it — just by finishing this chapter."

CHAPTER 17: THE WEALTH GAME – MASTERING STRATEGY, NOT JUST TACTICS

◈ Tex Talks:

"Most people hustle for money. The wealthy position for power. This isn't a game of dice—it's chess. And it's your move."

I. What Game Are You Playing?

Let's get something straight: Wealth is a game.

But like all games, there are levels. Some people are playing checkers. Others are playing poker. The elite? They're playing chess on a hundred boards at once.

You've been taught:

- To earn a paycheck (tactic)
- To budget wisely (tactic)
- To save for retirement (tactic)

But here's what you weren't taught:

- How to position capital
- How to leverage debt with precision
- How to turn relationships into revenue streams

The wealthy aren't smarter—they're better trained. They were raised in boardrooms, not break rooms. They were given frameworks, not fear.

You're not behind—you're just stepping into the game now.

II. Strategy vs. Tactics: The Critical Distinction

Tactics win moments. Strategy wins empires.

Tactics	Strategy
Cutting spending	Building a passive income stream
Buying one stock	Designing a portfolio to weather all markets
Working overtime	Buying equity in the company
Chasing trends	Creating long-term pricing power

◈ Tex Reminder:

"If you're still trading time for money, you're playing the wrong game."

A good tactic without a strategy is like a pawn moving without a plan—destined to fall.

III. My Playbook: From Grassroots to Global Capital

Let's talk real moves.

When I was 12 years old, I launched Kiss My Grass Landscaping—yes, that was the name. I:

- Negotiated the contracts
- Hired my friends
- Managed the books
- Sold the company for six figures before I ever stepped foot on a college campus

That wasn't luck. That was early strategy:

- Build a recurring service business
- Lock in institutional clients
- Scale with low labor cost
- Exit before overhead crushes margins

By the time I was at Wharton, I didn't need case studies. I'd lived them.

Today, with over $700 million in assets under management through Carbonado Capital, I still apply the same principles:

- Know your edge
- Leverage it without apology
- Play long—not loud

IV. The 4 Pillars of Strategic Wealth Building

Let me break it down. Strategy in wealth is built on four immovable pillars:

1. Vision

This isn't vague "see yourself rich" nonsense.

It's defining where your money, time, and power need to be in 10, 20, and 50 years.

Questions to ask:

- Where do I want my family living in 2045?
- What income streams must exist without me?
- Who do I want to control influence over?

Without vision, you're just reacting. With vision, you're engineering.

---

2. Leverage

Wealth is not built with hard work alone—it's built with leverage.

Types of leverage:

- Capital – Making your money work harder than you do
- People – Hiring or partnering with the right minds
- Technology – Automating systems that don't sleep
- Debt – Used responsibly, it's a weapon of mass wealth

◈ Tex Truth:

"I've built companies with my mind, not my muscles. Leverage is the billionaire's protein powder."

3. Timing

It's not just what you buy. It's when.

- Bought real estate in 2010? You're golden.
- Bought NFTs in 2021? Good luck.

The game rewards those who read cycles—not headlines.

◈ Pro move: Learn macroeconomic indicators.

When interest rates shift, everything else follows. Wealthy people don't just look at the market—they study it.

4. Network

The rich don't invest in stocks. They invest in people.

Your network is:

- A pipeline for opportunity
- A shield against downside
- A compass for decisions

Build it with intention. Every quarter, audit your circle:

- Who brings value?
- Who costs you energy or clarity?
- Who's playing at the level you're aiming for?

The game is faster, sharper, and safer when you're not alone.

V. The Opponent: Consumer Culture and Comfort

Don't be naïve. You have an opponent—and it isn't the IRS or the market.

It's the system that teaches you to consume instead of control.

You were trained:

- To lease, not own
- To react, not plan
- To survive, not scale

But here's the truth: comfort is a sedative.

You'll never dominate the wealth game if you're addicted to convenience.

Burn the idea that wealth is supposed to be easy. It's not. But it's worth it.

VI. The Case Study: The Dentist and the Truck Driver

Let me give you two real clients:

Dr. Angela (The Dentist)

- Makes $400K/year
- Drives a Tesla
- Vacation home in Vail
- Net worth? $212K

Why?

- High expenses
- Poor investments
- No strategy—just income

Earl (Truck Driver, 3rd shift)

- Makes $85K/year
- Owns four rental properties
- Invests 40% of income
- Net worth? $1.6 million

Why?

- Strategic asset building
- High savings rate
- Clear legacy goal

◈ Tex Insight:
"The money you earn is your fuel. The strategy you follow is your engine."

VII. The Wealth Playbook Challenge

Let's move from knowledge to power.

Do this now:

1. Draw your game board.

Four boxes: Vision | Leverage | Timing | Network
Fill in your current assets in each.

1. Write your Wealth Playbook Rule #1:

"I no longer play to survive. I play to scale."

1. Audit your last 5 financial decisions:
    - Were they tactical or strategic?
    - Did they move you toward sovereignty?
2. Set a 90-Day Strategic Move:
    - Invest in your first real estate asset
    - Launch a digital product
    - Join a network that earns 10x your level

◈ Tex Final Word:

"You weren't born to play defense. You were born to build dynasties. Learn the rules. Build your strategy. Then flip the board and run the table."

Chapter 18: Execution is Everything – Turning Knowledge Into Capital

◈ Tex Talks:

"Information is cheap. Execution is rare. In the real world, talkers lose. Executors win. It's that simple."

In every prison yard, boardroom, and back alley I've been through, one law is always true: you don't rise to your goals—you fall to your habits. This chapter isn't about what you know—it's about what you do with what you know. Because the marketplace pays for performance, not potential.

I. The Myth of Information Alone

There's a dangerous lie floating around modern culture: that information equals wealth. That reading enough books, bingeing enough podcasts, or watching enough gurus on YouTube somehow entitles you to financial success.

But I've seen men with degrees from Ivy League schools who are flat broke—and hustlers with high school diplomas who run million-dollar portfolios.

The truth? Knowledge is potential. Execution is kinetic.

Reading about compound interest won't make you rich. But automating weekly investments into your portfolio will. Understanding real estate depreciation won't buy you a single door—but negotiating your first property with a seller will.

◈ Tex Talks:

"Most people are drowning in knowledge and starving for results."

II. Why Execution Is the Currency of the Wealthy

What separates the wealthy isn't just what they know. It's what they're willing to do, repeatedly, without applause.

- JThey don't "plan to start." They start small and scale.
- They don't dream. They delegate, automate, and systematize.
- They don't react to the market. They build in every season—bull or bear.

If you want to change your financial life, don't just upgrade your ideas. Upgrade your follow-through.

Execution is a spiritual discipline. It requires self-mastery. Which is why most never achieve it.

III. The 3% Rule: Doing What You Know

Studies show the average person only applies about 3% of what they learn. That's tragic. But here's the flip side: you can outperform 97% of people simply by acting on what you already know.

You know you need to invest.

You know you need to track your spending.

You know you need to say no to lifestyle creep.

So why aren't you?

Fear? Perfectionism? Waiting for someone to hold your hand?

◈ Tex Talks:

"If you only act when conditions are perfect, you'll die broke."

IV. From Classroom to Cash Flow: Real-World Application

Let me show you what this looks like in practice.

Case 1: The Guy with All the Books

He could quote Buffett, knew P/E ratios backwards, and corrected people on finance forums. But he'd never opened a Roth IRA. He "was still researching."

Five years later—same story. No assets. Just analysis paralysis.

Case 2: The Woman with the Envelope

Single mom, three kids, two jobs. Took my workshop. Didn't fully understand compound growth—but understood discipline. She opened a brokerage account and auto-deposited $100 a month. Six years later? $11K portfolio and growing. She now owns her first duplex.

V. Building Your Personal Execution Plan

This is where the rubber meets the road.

Step 1: Choose ONE financial goal.

Not five. Not seven. ONE. Start with clarity. Maybe it's:

- Open a brokerage account
- Save $1,000 emergency fund
- Pay off a credit card

Step 2: Break it into a 7-day action.
Execution needs urgency. Examples:

- "Research and open a Fidelity account by Friday."
- "Set up automatic transfer of $25/week."
- "Call credit card company and negotiate APR."

Step 3: Put it on your calendar.
If it's not scheduled, it's not real.
Step 4: Track it. Publicly if needed.
Tell a friend. Use a whiteboard. Gamify your grind.
◈ Tex Talks:
"Execution is sexy. Consistency is divine."

VI. Legacy Builder Case Study: From Notes to Net Worth

Jeremiah, 25, formerly incarcerated, came to one of my finance workshops with nothing but a notebook and questions.

He had no credit, no job history, and no idea what a mutual fund was. But he acted:

1. Opened a secured credit card.
2. Started doing day labor and deposited 10% of every check.
3. Opened a brokerage account within 30 days.

4. Bought shares of Coca-Cola and Home Depot after reading their 10-Ks.

By year two, he had:

- A 742 credit score
- $13,000 saved
- His first car bought in cash
- His first investment property under contract

⟐ Tex Tribute:

"He didn't wait to be free to build wealth. He started with what he had."

VII. Action Plan: Turn Your Next Page into Your Next Paycheck

Here's your challenge:

⟐ Open your brokerage account NOW. Stop reading. Go. Do it.

⟐ Set up your auto-transfer. Start small. $10/week is fine.

⟐ Pick ONE company. Read their 10-K. Make one small investment.

⟐ Write your goal. "By [DATE], I will [specific financial goal] because [reason]."

Execution is what separates readers from millionaires.

⟐ Tex Talks:

"Reading this chapter won't make you rich. But doing what's in it just might."

Chapter 19: Financial Leadership – Building Generational Wealth on Purpose

◈ Tex Talks:

"A title doesn't make you a leader. Legacy does. And if your money dies with you, so does your impact."

I. Redefining Leadership Through a Financial Lens

Leadership isn't about commanding a room—it's about changing the future.

Real leadership means asking yourself: What happens when I'm gone?

If the answer is "nothing," you weren't leading. You were surviving.

Financial leadership is legacy in motion. It's not about the car you drive, the suit you wear, or how many zeros are in your account. It's about how many lives you elevate with the systems, values, and assets you leave behind.

This isn't just about passing down wealth. It's about passing down wisdom.

II. Generational Wealth Is a System, Not a Slogan

Let's kill a myth: Generational wealth isn't just owning things. It's owning a system that produces income, knowledge, and opportunity long after you're gone.

That means:

- Trusts, not just savings.
- Operating businesses, not just jobs.
- Financial literacy baked into family culture, not just annual "money talks."

◈ Tex Talks:

"I don't just want my children wealthy—I want them wise. Because untrained heirs become broke adults."

III. The Family Operating System

Think of your household like a company—with a name, a mission, and a strategy.

◈ Family Constitution

What values govern your house? What's non-negotiable? Write it down. Frame it.

◈ Financial SOPs (Standard Operating Procedures)

- 10% of income gets invested.
- Credit cards are paid in full monthly.
- No large purchases without a 48-hour wait period.
- Monthly money meetings.

◈ Education Pipeline

You don't wait for schools to teach your kids compound interest. You teach it at the dinner table.

◈ Tex Talks:

"If Walmart has a business plan and your family doesn't... who's running the smarter operation?"

IV. Ownership Is the Goal

Assets—not just income—must be the target.

Jobs pay bills. Ownership builds empires.

- Real estate: Rental income, equity, leverage
- Stocks: Dividend cash flow, capital appreciation
- Businesses: Tax advantages, multi-generational control

Ownership gives your family the one thing money alone never will: autonomy.

Don't just teach your children how to earn. Teach them how to own.

V. The "Three Generations" Curse – And How to Beat It

You've heard the pattern:

- Generation 1 sacrifices and builds.
- Generation 2 maintains and enjoys.
- Generation 3 squanders it all.

Why? Because most families pass down assets without passing down mindsets.

You beat this curse by:

1. Normalizing hard conversations about wealth and death.
2. Putting financial training in your estate plan.
3. Making values more valuable than valuables.

◈ Tex Talks:

"Don't just give them the key—teach them how to run the kingdom."

VI. Case Study: The Brooks Family Blueprint

The Brooks family, based out of Tulsa, wasn't wealthy—yet. But after attending one of my workshops, they built a 25-year generational wealth plan.

- Started an LLC to run their side businesses
- Bought a duplex and made the kids co-owners
- Created a family trust
- Monthly family financial dinners with vision boards

Result? By year 5:

- Their 17-year-old daughter filed her first tax return as a business owner
- Their 12-year-old son pitched and won a youth

entrepreneurship award
- Their family net worth jumped from $42K to $618K

That's financial leadership.

VII. Action Plan: Create Your Generational Wealth Manifesto

◈ Step 1: Write Your Family's Financial Vision Statement.

Example: "We are the Thomas family. We own. We invest. We give. We leave no generation behind."

◈ Step 2: Set 3 Financial Commandments.

These are non-negotiables. Example:

- "Debt is for leverage, not lifestyle."
- "Every dollar has a job."
- "We invest before we spend."

◈ Step 3: Build Your Legacy Team.

- CPA
- Estate planner
- Financial coach
- Accountability partners

◈ Step 4: Have the Talk.

Yes, that talk. The uncomfortable one. Assets. Wills. Death. Inheritance. Stewardship.

If you won't, someone else will—probably the IRS.

◈ Tex Talks:

"You're not just building wealth. You're building warriors. Train them. Equip them. Send them forward."

Chapter 20: Legacy Over Luxury – The Final Move That Matters

◈ Tex Talks:

"I've worn the tailored suits. I've closed eight-figure deals. But when I'm gone, none of that matters if I didn't build something that outlives me."

I. The Real Flex Is Legacy

Let's settle something: Luxury isn't the goal. Legacy is.

Luxury is loud. Legacy is built in silence and revealed in time.

Luxury says, "Look at what I have."

Legacy says, "Let me show you what I left."

You don't need another Rolex. You need a reason.

The world doesn't remember what car you drove. It remembers what impact you made.

And wealth without purpose? That's just glitter on a hollow crown.

II. Why Most Wealth Disappears Within a Generation

According to the Institute for Family Studies:

- 70% of generational wealth disappears by the second generation
- 90% is gone by the third

Not because they didn't have assets—but because they didn't have alignment.

No mission. No mentorship. No map.

That ends with you.

◈ Tex Talks:

"You're not building a castle—they burn. You're building culture. That's eternal."

III. Define Your Legacy, Don't Leave It to Chance

Legacy isn't what you leave behind. It's what you send ahead.

You don't wait until your deathbed to define it. You build it now:

- In your investments
- In your mentorship
- In your children's discipline
- In your family's rituals
- In your community footprint

Ask yourself:

- What principles should guide my family 100 years from now?
- What systems will keep them free when I'm gone?
- What impact will my name evoke?

If you don't script that story, the world will write a different one—and it won't honor you.

IV. Faith, Freedom, and the Final Investment

I didn't just write this book for people with brokerage accounts.

I wrote this for:

- The man rebuilding from nothing.
- The woman who said no to poverty and yes to ownership.
- The young leader who's breaking generational chains.
- The incarcerated mind with the millionaire spirit.

◈ Tex Talks:

"I've seen God flip failure into fuel. That's why I give. That's why I build. That's why I fight."

The final investment isn't your money.

It's your time, your influence, your why.

Make that investment count.

V. Your Final Challenge: The Legacy Letter

Do this now. Not tomorrow. Not someday.

Write a one-page letter to your future great-grandchild.

Answer these questions:

1. What did you stand for?
2. What did you build and why?
3. What principles do you want them to live by?
4. What do you hope they will build next?

Sign it. Date it. Seal it. That's your first true asset.

◈ Tex Talks:

"The markets will rise and fall. But the values you leave—they're recession-proof."

Final Words from Big Tex

I've been broke. I've been wealthy. I've led towns. I've sat in prison. I've earned my degrees, built my companies, raised my daughters, and outlived my doubters.

But none of that matters unless you take what's in this book and run with it.

Not just to the bank. But into your future.

This isn't just a financial manual—it's a declaration:

> You are no longer waiting for wealth. You are building it.
>
> You are no longer watching legacy happen. You are living it.
>
> You are no longer asking permission. You are claiming what's yours.

Welcome to the other side.

◈ Tex Final Word:

"Wealth isn't a number. It's a narrative. And starting today, you're the author."

A Personal Letter from Gregory A. Thomas

Dear Reader,

Thank you.

Not just for reading Wealth Starts Here, but for doing something far more important: investing in yourself.

You could've spent your time anywhere—scrolling headlines, chasing distractions, settling for the same cycle. But instead, you opened these pages. You leaned in. You made the choice to learn, to grow, and to lead. And for that, I honor you.

I didn't write this book to impress. I wrote it to ignite.

Because I know what it feels like to start with nothing but an idea and a will to win. I've seen both sides of the ledger—success and setback, boardroom and cellblock, overflow and overdraft. And if there's one truth I've earned the right to shout, it's this:

> You don't need permission to build wealth. You just need a decision.

A decision to stop letting life happen to you... and start taking ownership of your time, your dollars, your mindset, and your future.

It doesn't matter if you're 18 or 81.

Doesn't matter if you're free or behind bars, rich or rebuilding.

You can start now. You can start small. But for God's sake—just start.

Because wealth isn't about flexing.

It's about freedom.

It's about options.

It's about leaving something better behind than what you inherited.

So as you close this book, don't just put it on a shelf.

Put it into motion.

Build your first budget.

Buy that first stock.

Open that investment account.

Teach someone else what you've learned.

Make one move—then another. And another.

Because movement compounds faster than money ever will.

And when doubt creeps in—and it will—remember this:

> You are not broke. You are becoming.
>
> You are not behind. You are building.
>
> You are not waiting. You are working.

Wealth starts where you are.

It starts with what you have.

It starts right now.

With deepest respect and unwavering belief in your journey,

Gregory A. Thomas

aka Big Tex

About the Author

Dr. Gregory A. Thomas is not just a financial strategist—he's a movement. Known to many as Big Tex, he is a nationally respected economist, entrepreneur, publishing executive, and former elected official whose life and leadership defy conventional boundaries.

Dr. Thomas holds a Ph.D. in Economics from The Wharton School, an MBA from Southern Methodist University, and dual bachelor's degrees in Political Science and Marketing from the University of Texas. He also earned dual doctorates in Theology and Ministry from The King's University.

He is the Founder and Advisory Partner of Carbonado Capital Investments, overseeing more than $700 million in assets under management, and the Chief Operating Officer of multiple successful ventures, including Global Hair 4U, Heated Armor, and Thomas Family Ranches, Inc. Through Thomas & Thomas Publishing House, he continues to elevate new voices and publish transformational works that blend faith, finance, and leadership.

A former two-term Town Councilman and the youngest Mayor in the history of Heath, Texas, Dr. Thomas has spent his life building bridges between policy, purpose, and the people. Even while incarcerated, he continues to lead financial literacy workshops, author books, publish curriculum, and mentor men behind the wire.

Wealth Starts Here is more than a book—it's a testament to his calling. Through it, Dr. Thomas empowers readers to reclaim their economic power, think like owners, and build wealth from wherever they are.

He lives by the belief:

"Ownership is the foundation of freedom—and wealth is a decision."

Read more at www.gregoryathomas.com.

About the Publisher

Gregory A. Thomas Enterprises is a premier publishing and intellectual property firm dedicated to producing bold, transformative works that challenge systems, spark dialogue, and empower readers across disciplines. Founded by economist, entrepreneur, and bestselling author Dr. Gregory A. Thomas, the enterprise operates at the intersection of scholarship, strategy, and social impact.

With a sharp focus on truth-telling, innovation, and integrity, Gregory A. Thomas Enterprises specializes in publishing books that expose hidden power structures, demystify complex ideas, and amplify voices committed to justice, reform, and financial literacy. The company curates a dynamic catalogue of nonfiction, political commentary, faith-based works, and economic thought leadership—delivered with unmatched clarity and conviction.

Backed by a multidisciplinary team of editors, strategists, and designers, the firm offers a full-service publishing experience with uncompromising quality. From concept development to global distribution, Gregory A. Thomas Enterprises exists to elevate serious ideas and bold authors who are unafraid to disrupt the status quo.

More than a publishing house—it is a movement in print.

More than books—it is legacy-building through language.

www.ingramcontent.com/pod-product-compliance
Lightning Source LLC
LaVergne TN
LVHW052249200926
848481LV00002B/320
* 9 7 9 8 2 3 1 4 8 6 5 3 3 *